What Others Are Saying about *Hard Ball on Holy Ground*

"The mission of our Church is to make disciples of Jesus Christ. In order to make disciples we must first live as disciples by treating others with the love and respect exemplified in Jesus. We are challenged to be the body of Christ and to live in loving community, yet there are those in our midst who constantly seek ways to weaken the body and destroy the structure. This book will reveal the motives and tactics being used by some individuals and groups as they seek to re-define our faith and our witness."

— Marilyn J. Outslay
Delegate to three UMC General Conferences
Lay Delegate to British Methodist Conference

"Determining the truth as seen by those in disagreement is a major problem. Discovering the 'whole truth' is nearly impossible. However, the contents of this book makes a persuasive effort to set things straight regarding the critics of The United Methodist Church."

— Keith Pohl
Former editor of Circuit Rider magazine

"Understanding what our values are, articulating why these are our values, and then putting them into practice in our daily lives is vital for good mental health. Doing the same on the national and global levels is vital to good spiritual health. By doing this, we can live consciously and make choices based on what we really believe. Divisiveness, polarization, intolerance, attacking others, vilifying those with differing opinions, and outright lying have become effective political weapons of late. We have seen this in the politics of our country, and now also in the politics of religion – politics that have become inextricably and dangerously entwined with government politics. People who believe in the goodness and healing power of love, compassion, tolerance, inclusion, justice, respect, and unity would be well advised to educate themselves on the issues presented in *Hard Ball on Holy Ground.* Being ignorant and silent about these issues is not a responsible choice."

– Charlene Hosenfeld, Ph.D
Clinical Psychologist and Presbyterian Church member, Kailua, Hawaii

---

"This book needs to be read by all who are concerned about the integrity and effectiveness of the Christian witness in today's world. In various, telling ways, these essays and interviews show how several extremist groups, under the guise of 'orthodoxy,' are attempting to hijack for their own purposes the United Methodist, Episcopal, and Presbyterian traditions, especially. The essays that describe the aims and methods of these groups provide illuminating historical and theological commentary, as well as factual data. Ironically, the essays intended as rejoinders will strike many readers as verifying much of what the critics claim."

– Victor Paul Furnish
University Distinguished Professor of New Testament, Emeritus
Perkins School of Theology, Southern Methodist University

"Church renewal should mean that we grow in faithfulness to the Gospel. It should mean a new embrace of the biblical vision of reconciliation and peace. So why are some so-called advocates of mainline church 'renewal' actually undermining the churches' witness for peace and justice in our society? You will find well-researched answers to this troubling question in *Hard Ball on Holy Ground.* Methodists, Presbyterians, Episcopalians and others will be dismayed to learn that the churches they love are targets of a campaign of destabilization, but we ignore this reality at our peril."

– Dr. Bob Edgar
General Secretary, National Council of Churches USA

"As the co-Chairperson of *United Methodism@Risk,* a detailed study of the right-wing attacks upon the Church, I heartily endorse this volume. I signed on to the *@Risk* project because as a bishop of the Church I served for eight years as a Director of the General Board of Global

Ministries, followed by four years as a part-time consultant on African Development. Throughout those years I observed a relentless disinformation campaign flowing from the 'Renewal' groups who seek to discredit the witness of faithful servants of the Gospel serving around the world. Leading mission study groups through 42 countries over the years, I saw the effect on the morale of our missionaries and leaders of our partner churches, who often asked: 'Who are these people?' This volume answers that question."

– Bishop C. Dale White
United Methodist Bishop (retired)

"United Methodists are faced with hard choices today: Do we dare to embrace theological development and social transformation, or will we cling to doctrinal security and institutional maintenance? If we hope to preserve the unity of our United Methodist Church, while remaining true to the best elements of our Wesleyan heritage, knowledge is essential–knowledge of the measures being used to drive us apart, the history behind them, and who is using them. *Hard Ball on Holy Ground* provides that education–detailed information on what is confronting us and how we are challenged to speak the truth in love boldly, today as never before. I particularly appreciate the inclusion of statements from both ends of the progessive/conservative spectrum, allowing key individuals to speak for themselves. This volume is a constructive tool for navigation through these critical times."

– M. Theresa Basile
Co-President, Methodist Federation for Social Action (California-Pacific Chapter)

"This collection of articles sheds helpful light on the nature of the heated controversy embroiling the United Methodist and other mainline churches. Ignoring the problem is not an option for serious church members. I strongly recommend it be used as a companion resource with *United Methodism @ Risk: A Wake Up Call* for individual and group study."

– Eloise M. Cranke
First UMC Des Moines Iowa,layperson

Hard Ball
on
Holy Ground

Boston Wesleyan Press

To Rhett Jackson
with appreciation
for his Christian
conscience and courage

Hard Ball
on
Holy Ground

The Religious Right v. the Mainline
for the Church's Soul

STEPHEN SWECKER
Editor

Boston Wesleyan Press

Library of Congress Control Number: 2005903168

ISBN: 0-9711146-2-5

The BW Press
P.O. Box 458
North Berwick, ME 03906

Printed in the United States of America

CONTENTS

PREFACE   v
Stephen Swecker

FOREWORD   vii
John B. Cobb, Jr.

Playing Hard Ball on Holy Ground   1
J. Philip Wogaman

Follow the Money: Documenting the Right's   6
Well-heeled Assault on the UMC (with Addendum)
Andrew J. Weaver and Nicole Seibert

Response: Interview with Mark Tooley   29

Embedded: Charting the IRD's Ties to the Radical Right   36
Nicole Seibert and Andrew J. Weaver

Purveyors of False Memory: Unmasking   40
the Institute on Religion and Democracy
Thom White Wolf Fassett

Response: Open Churches Welcome Dissent   48
Diane Knippers and Mark Tooley

When Good News Is Bad News,   58
or Working on a Coup D'etat
Andrew J. Weaver, Nicole Seibert and Fred Kandeler

Response: A Good News Response to Recent Accusations   69

Crashing the Farewell Party   76
Linda S. Rhodes

The Ominous Cost of 'Renewal'   80
Andrew J. Weaver

Why the Right Proposed Schism   82
Scott Campbell

Interview: Diane Knippers   87
Stephen Swecker

Stealthy Zinger   101
Stephen Swecker

PREFACE

What is going on? Answering that question is the
first requirement of responsible decision-making
and acting, according to theologian H. Richard
Niebuhr (*The Responsible Self*, 1963). The reason
is evident: Responsible behavior is all-but-impossible if it does
not begin with an accurate understanding of what is–what, in
other words, is actually happening.

What follows, therefore, is a modest effort toward that end
regarding the current situation facing Christian faith communities at the beginning of the 21st century. This volume presents a
selection of articles–research, essays and interviews–that can be
regarded as primary source material for anyone trying to answer
the following question:

What is going on in the interaction between right-wing forces
in the secular and religious worlds and the institutions of mainline Christianity, particularly The United Methodist Church?
Only when we have answered that question are we prepared to
address what might be regarded as the second question of

responsible Christian behavior: What am I, as a follower of Jesus Christ and a member of his church, to do? (Paul L. Lehmann, *Ethics in a Christian Context*, 1963)

An understandable interest exists in "doing" something by those for whom the tactics and goals of the Right are cause for alarm; we share that interest to a considerable degree. But an ethic of responsibility counsels us to learn as much as we can about the situation we would "correct" rather than starting with an ideological presumption that anything our side does is automatically a fitting response.

A word of explanation about this volume: It offers no grand theory about the "hard ball" institutional conflict experienced by mainline churches during the last 30 years. The articles were not conceived or written in concert with each other. Rather, they were published separately in the magazine that I edit, Zion's Herald, its Internet counterpart, ZH World (www.zhworld.net), or elsewhere. The order in which they appear has the minimum virtue of a *beginning*–a theme-setting chapter by J. Philip Wogaman; a *middle*–the bulk of the book, consisting of research, reports and interviews that illustrate the situation; and an *ending*–an essay by the editor that offers a concluding overview. The volume's overall outlook is guided by a perception of right-wing efforts to undermine the effectiveness of mainline denominations. But a deliberate attempt is made to include voices of those whose actions are critiqued–an essential component of any responsible effort to discern what is going on.

The Foreword by John B. Cobb, Jr., contributes an original comprehensive summary of how mainline churches in the U.S. arrived at where we are today. I commend Dr. Cobb's essay as an invaluable starting point for reading and thinking about the materials in this volume. Among other things, as an historical overview, it provides clues to "what is going on" that can help open the discussion for wider debate and reflection–as, we hope, the various contents of this small volume will also do.

– STEPHEN SWECKER

FOREWORD

JOHN B. COBB, Jr.

I
t is news to none of us that The United Methodist Church is in crisis. This is not the first time. Groups have broken off from its parent denominations more than once, and it split over slavery on geographical lines.

One element in the present crisis seems new and, to those who are its victims, particularly offensive. This time an external organization, composed chiefly of people who do not stand in the Wesleyan tradition, is playing a leadership role in exacerbating the disagreements within the denomination. Further, this organization, the Institute on Religion and Democracy, is funded chiefly by people whose interests are primarily political and economic. For them, changing the leadership and public voice of the mainline denominations is part of a broader undertaking to silence all effective forms of progressive opposition to the rightist turn in national policy.

It often seems that, while the wedge issues the IRD uses to garner support within the denomination are doctrinal and moral, its real interest is to change the nature of our social witness. This social witness expresses the deep-seated conviction of many who stand in the tradition of John Wesley that the church should side with the poor and oppressed against the rich and powerful. The denominational leadership is accustomed to affirming public responsibility to maintain and expand services to the poor and to strengthen their voice in public life. Accordingly, it typically criticizes the current curtailing and dismantling of such pro-grams. Those who favor this dismantling find this role of the church an objectionable interference in their quest for still greater control over national policies. They would be happy if the public voice of the church were directed only to maintaining traditional personal morality. They are willing to put large resources into effecting these changes.

The IRD has targeted not only United Methodists but also the Presbyterian Church (USA) and the Episcopalians. It brings to the task financial resources that are very large in comparison with the sums usually available to dissident factions in church disputes. Its methods are sophisticated and effective. Its work has already weakened the public voice of these denominations. It has also aroused increasing resentment on the part of denom-inational leaders who are targeted for disempowerment—and on the part of the many others who, through normal institu-tional channels, have placed them in positions of leadership.

Only recently, however, has there been any sustained effort to counter the work of the IRD. This effort has consisted chiefly of making the nature and role of the IRD more visible to a larger segment of the church membership. Those engaged in this effort believe that many church members, even those who are often critical of positions taken by leadership, do not want the denominations to become tools of the secular political and eco-nomic right. To understand where we now are it may help to consider, very briefly, where we have been and how our present disagreements arose.

Through much of the nineteenth and twentieth centuries,

what were then "the mainline churches" both expressed and informed the mainstream of American life. They were "conservative" in the sense that they cherished both the Christian heritage and traditional American ideals, which they understood to be closely related to this heritage. They took for granted the authority of the Bible, but they were tolerant of diversity of interpretation and application, and they recognized in each other valid expressions of the Christian faith. Increasingly, they sought to work together harmoniously rather than to compete. They also supported the separation of church and state so as to give space to religious communities that were not Christian.

The mainline churches increasingly affirmed democracy and education and medical care for all. Although they long reflected the racism of American society, they tended to recognize a tension between their Christian heritage and their acceptance of slavery and, later, of segregation, so that they finally supported emancipation and desegregation. Their Christian and democratic commitments opened them to sensitivity about the exploitation of workers during the industrial revolution and, later, of other minority groups.

They believed that the form of Christianity they had developed in this country could benefit people everywhere, spiritually, morally, socially, and physically. They strongly supported the great missionary movement of the nineteenth century. This expanded their horizons of sensitivity and understanding, especially among their female members. Partly for this reason, the mainline churches leaned toward international cooperation rather than isolationism or American imperialism.

These churches understood their Christian beliefs to be the truth about the world. This did not mean, however, that they closed themselves to scholarly and scientific developments. On the contrary, it meant that they were ready to have their beliefs tested in free interchange. Accordingly, they encouraged education and supported freedom of research. They were prepared to adjust Christian teaching to what was demonstrated by historians as well as scientists. This meant that, toward the end of the nineteenth century, they admitted historical criticism of the Bible into their seminaries and came to terms with the scientific discoveries about evolution. During the same period, and partly as a result of the new scholarly study of the Bible, they gave greater emphasis to issues of justice and peace in the public world.

These three developments in the late nineteenth century introduced still unresolved tensions into the life of the churches in the twentieth century. The theology that emerges from reading the Bible as critical historians differs from the theology that results from reading it only through the eyes of a tradition that has treated it as a sacred text. The theology that emerges from accepting dominant scientific theories differs from that which takes the Bible as a source for scientific knowledge. And the theology that sees discipleship to Jesus as calling for a quest for justice for all differs from one that focuses almost exclusively on personal salvation and moral obedience.

The Modernist/Fundamentalist controversy split some denominations. However, the mainstream sought a middle way in which criticism was allowed without dethroning Scripture as the sacred text of the church. It accepted scientific findings while segregating them into a field separate from that of Christian faith. It recognized the importance of working for justice while maintaining a strong focus on the spiritual needs of individuals and families. These compromises avoided fracturing of the mainstream denominations, but the compromise is fully satisfactory to few.

For the most part, those church people who gave the most attention to these issues and were best educated about them took critical study of the scriptures seriously, accepted the findings of the sciences, and recognized the centrality in the Bible of the call to justice in public affairs. That meant that most of the church leadership moved in this direction. However, many members were hardly aware of these developments and certainly did not draw the consequences. The leadership, including local pastors, was theologically fragmented. It did not do well in drawing the majority of church members into theological discussion. Instead, it tended to avoid controversial topics. As a result, the gap between leadership and much of the membership grew wider and wider.

As new leaders emerged who understood the issues but rejected the direction taken by the majority of their peers, the situation changed. These conservatives were able to arouse feelings of resentment on the part of many members. These members felt, to some extent rightly, that their way of understanding the faith had been viewed condescendingly. Their faithful support of the church had been exploited for purposes that were in tension with their own. For example, they were supporting seminaries that were influencing future pastors in directions that moved away from what the donors considered to be Christian.

The majority of members of the mainstream denominations recognized that their leaders needed to deal with problems that required specialized knowledge, and they were willing to trust them to do this responsibly. However, the leaders who opposed the dominant direction taken by the denominations on these basic matters were able to persuade many members to give up that trust and redirect their energies to opposition. Thus the rise of organized and effective opposition is an understandable development within the mainstream denominations, especially as it is strongly supported by the general drift of the culture to the right.

There is, thus, a deep divide in our mainstream denominations. On the one side are those who want to continue, and strengthen, the broadly liberal program of taking historical study of the Bible seriously, affirming the freedom of science and the need for Christians to accept the authority of scientists in their own fields, and working for justice in the public sphere as well as in the church. On the other side are those who want to maintain the historic teachings of the church little changed even when they come into conflict with scientific findings and who believe that the church should focus on the personal salvation of individuals and their personal morality, leaving issues of public policy to others.

Of course, many members hold views that do not fit this classification neatly. For example, there are persons who are minimally influenced by biblical criticism who still hear the Bible's call for justice in the public world and who strongly support the church's effort to speak and act for the poor and oppressed. On the other side, there are those who are quite concerned to be shaped in their thinking by the latest biblical scholarship and the latest scientific developments, but have little time for questions of justice. I myself belong to a group that believes the social and natural sciences are too important to be left to specialists in those fields and that Christian faith can and should be brought to bear in the formulation of their findings.

Part of the hope for the future is that we need not forever be stuck in the divide that I outlined above. Nevertheless, at present that dual classification has considerable relevance.

Thus far I have not even mentioned the dominant presenting issue that has brought these underlying differences to the surface: homosexuality. It is not, of course, the case that all who accept biblical criticism, the results of scientific inquiry, and the commitment to justice favor church recognition of same-sex unions and the ordination of gays and lesbians who are otherwise qualified. Nor is it the case that those who have not followed these late 19th-century developments are all against such policies. But in general there are close connections, and these make dialogue between the two groups difficult.

These problems are not the result of meddling by the Institute on Religion and Democracy. But they have been intentionally exacerbated by its involvement. Whereas those who are chiefly informed by their inherited faith seek mutual respect and understanding across the divide and cooperation on other matters where agreement is possible, the work of the IRD is to intensify suspicion of the Christian integrity of denominational leadership. The goal of its donors is not the strengthening of united witness but the weakening of any resistance to the rightward swing of American politics, especially on matters of economics.

Whether there could be true reconciliation without the interference of the IRD remains uncertain. But for the faithful membership of the churches on both sides of the issues noted above, it is important to understand the role the IRD is playing and to avoid being co-opted by it. Reading this small volume will help in the process of distinguishing legitimate Christian differences from the distortions introduced by the interference of those whose agenda are not those of any responsible Christian body.

Hard Ball on Holy Ground

Playing Hard Ball on Holy Ground

J. PHILIP WOGAMAN

I t is no secret that The United Methodist Church and other mainline denominations are faced with serious internal conflicts. That, in itself, is not necessarily bad. When in all the history of Christianity have Christians not had church fights of one kind or another? These can deal with doctrine, or polity, or practice or simply clashes of personality. In our humanness, we are prone to disagree. Disagreements, faced honestly and charitably, can lead us all to better practices and clearer understandings of theological truth.

But, I find it more disturbing that there are those within the church who want to fight using direct institutional power. In the difficult and sensitive issues related to homosexuality, for instance, pastors have been brought up on trial for actions of conscience that are contrary to church law. The Rev. Jimmy Creech was tried in Nebraska for conducting a same-gender commitment ceremony and deprived of his credentials. The Rev. Greg Dell was similarly tried in Chicago, given a limited suspen-

1

sion and re-admitted upon his commitment to stay within church law. The Rev. Donald Fado and 67 other ministers in the California-Nevada Conference were investigated for a similar offense, but that proved to be too many ministers to act against!

A case can certainly be made that actions against church law must be dealt with by the church's disciplinary processes. But doesn't that raise the prior question whether the conduct of same-gender commitment ceremonies should be prohibited by church law? It wasn't prohibited by The United Methodist Church prior to 1996. Why did conservatives in the denomination feel it was so necessary to use the "hard ball" of church law and trials to make their point? Why couldn't they respect the conscience of those pastors–by all accounts, each was a very good one. Why could this not have been treated as one of those issues on which we try to persuade one another?

At least, why did the penalty sought through the trial process have to be the elimination of a good pastor from ministry? What real harm had these pastors done?

Even as these questions dangled before the church, a group of 28 conservative clergy and laity from 11 annual conferences filed charges against Bishop C. Joseph Sprague of Chicago–not for actions contrary to church law but, allegedly, for teachings contrary to church doctrine. The group maintained that an address by Bishop Sprague at Iliff Theological Seminary in Denver in early 2002 and a book published by him in 2003 contained material contrary to essential United Methodist beliefs. The group's spokesperson, the Rev. Thomas Lambrecht of Greenville, Wisconsin, was quoted as saying that, "in his address and book, Bishop Sprague appears to deny the apostolic, orthodox, and ecumenical Trinitarian understanding of Jesus as God in favor of a form of Unitarianism or 'adoptionism' that denies the virgin birth and full deity of Christ."

Moreover, Mr. Lambrecht added, "He denies the physical resurrection of Christ's body. He maintains that Jesus Christ is not the only way to salvation and appears to deny the substitutionary atonement of Christ through his sacrificial death on the cross." (Source: United Methodist Communications)

So here we have a group bent upon resolving a theological disagreement, not by reason and dialogue, but by a crude exercise of institutional power. Their aim: to compel the bishop to recant his views or face a judicial proceeding. It didn't come to that, since the investigating panel to whom the charges were referred had the good sense to dismiss the complaint. Still, such power plays distract responsible leaders unreasonably and unnecessarily, and send a chilling message that there are groups prepared to play "hard ball" in the life of the church.

Times of rapid social and cultural change often bring on fears of the unknown and unfamiliar. It is perfectly understandable that numbers of people within and beyond the churches lose confidence in the persuasive power of the gospel and seek instead to use institutional power to shore up the faith once and for all delivered to the saints. My larger concern is with those who play upon such fears.

A recent editorial by James V. Heidinger II, editor of Good News magazine, illustrates the point. Referring to the responsibility of bishops and pastors to be "gatekeepers"–itself a revealing metaphor–Heidinger writes that "in every age, the church is threatened by those outside who would harm and destroy, and by those within who would accommodate the church to secular norms or harm the faithful by teaching false doctrine." He concludes that "many are deeply distressed when a United Methodist bishop denies publicly and without apology the classic understandings of Jesus' full and unique deity, his virgin birth, blood atonement, and bodily resurrection–and does so while lecturing authoritatively to future ministers studying at one of our UM seminaries."

This thinly-veiled reference to Bishop Sprague may give us some idea of the role played by organizations like Good News, the Confessing Movement, and the Institute on Religion and Democracy in the efforts to bring institutional pressure to bear upon leaders like Bishop Sprague. (The point is underscored in the Heidinger editorial by his praise for Cardinal Joseph Ratzinger. Cardinal Ratzinger is widely known for his efforts to silence such noted Roman Catholic theologians as Hans Kung, Charles Curran, and Edward Schillebeeckx. Do we want to replicate *that* in The United Methodist Church?)

There are, indeed, theological disputes among us. I can imagine some circumstances in which even a heresy trial might be in order. But, I know of no current bishop or other church leader for whom that would be remotely appropriate.

In Bishop Sprague's case, that would be singularly inappropriate. He is a deeply committed Christian with a gifted theological mind. I have read both the Iliff address and his recent book (*Affirmations of a Dissenter*, Abingdon 2003). It is obvious that some of his views do not coincide with those of the Good News Movement, the Institute on Religion and Democracy and the Confessing Movement. At most of the points of disagreement I'm with him and not with them. And yet, neither Bishop Sprague nor I would dream of filing charges against the leadership of those organizations or the 28 who have questioned his orthodoxy. That simply is not the way to resolve such disagreements.

I note in particular the complaint that he "denies the virgin birth." Indeed, Bishop Sprague's book thoughtfully discusses the origin of that part of the biblical narrative and explains why no Christian should be required to take it as literal fact. I do not know where all United Methodists stand on that now, but I feel certain that millions of them would be closer to Bishop Sprague on such questions than to his critics. The more important issue is where the truth lies.

The bishop voices his deep faith in the revelation of God's love through Christ. Shouldn't that be the center point? How one frames the deep faith in understandable terms may vary. The unique contribution of the "Wesleyan quadrilateral" is that it acknowledges the importance of four sources of theological insight: Scripture, tradition, experience and reason. That properly

4

restrains us from freezing any particular formulations for all time, and yet it keeps us grounded in the basic traditions of our faith.

The United Methodist Church and the other mainline denominations are not fundamentalist. A survey of Methodist views 40 years ago showed that less than ten percent were biblical literalists. Even amidst the religious insecurities of our time I doubt the figure would be any higher now. We have generally recognized that God is greater than any of us, always pushing us toward deeper understanding of the treasures of our faith. Endowed with reason, we are challenged to engage in serious dialogue within and beyond the church. Can we not trust the power of reason, grounded in faith, to see us through? Can we not allow the Holy Spirit to move our hearts in love?

What is to be said now to the strident voices tempting us to use raw power to resolve conflicts of mind and spirit? Surely the answer is that we cannot let harsh rhetoric and hard-ball tactics undermine mutual confidence and mutual respect in the life of the church. We should be more gentle in the church of Jesus Christ. We are on holy ground.

Follow the Money: Documenting the Right's Well-heeled Assault on the UMC

ANDREW WEAVER and NICOLE SEIBERT

During the summer of 2003, we reviewed an unsettling book titled *United Methodism @ Risk: A Wake Up Call* by Leon Howell (see Zion's Herald, July/August 2003). The book exposes an orchestrated attack by the American political and religious right on The United Methodist Church (UMC) and other mainline Protestant denominations that have been sufficiently vigorous, socially involved and politically effective to garner its wrath (Howell, 2003).

In response to the ensuing criticism of the book and our review, we organized a group of researchers to check the facts and found the volume to be well documented and reliable. In the process, we also reviewed hundreds of documents published by the key organization involved in the assault on the church, namely, the Institute on Religion and Democracy (IRD). Our findings as outlined below are very disturbing.

The IRD is affiliated with no denomination and is only accountable to its own self-appointed, self-perpetuating board

6

of directors. According to public sources, the IRD focuses its principal expenditures and most of its efforts on The United Methodist Church. In 2001, it spent $358,667 (46 percent of its total program expenditures) on "monitoring" the UMC's activities, leadership and public policy statements. In 1999, it spent $337,636 for the same purpose—more than six times what it spent on its "religious liberty" program that it declares in IRS documents to be its primary purpose (GuideStar, 2002).

From its inception in 1982, the IRD has been generously funded primarily by ultra-conservative organizations (Media Transparency, 2003). Records show that since it was founded, the IRD has received more than $1.9 million from the Scaife foundations, including an initial start-up grant of $200,000 (The Public Eye, 1989). The Scaife Family Foundations, managed by Richard Mellon Scaife, gave $225,000 to the IRD in 2002 for its "Reforming America's Churches Project" - among whose stated goals is the elimination of the UMC's General Board of Church and Society, the church's voice for justice and peace, as well as discrediting UMC pastors and bishops with whom they disagree by instigating church trials (Information Project for United Methodists, 2003). With respect to church trials, the IRD states the following in a fund-raising document to donors: "Over the next three years, we expect involvement in at least a dozen different cases around the country" (Institute on Religion and Democracy, 2001a).

The significance of the Scaife family's support of the IRD is best understood in the context of their foundations' overall pattern of funding. Richard Mellon Scaife, who controls the foundations' funds, is a billionaire who has subsidized many of the political right's formative institutions and organizations during the past 30 years (Rothmyer, 2000). His wealth was inherited from the Mellon banking and oil fortune.

In 1999 equivalent dollars, the Washington Post calculated that Mr. Scaife gave to conservative causes and institutions some $620 million during that 30-year period (Kaiser & Chinoy, 1999). In

7

the 1990s, Mr. Scaife supported groups with millions of dollars to fund lawsuits against the Clinton administration on a multitude of issues. In a revealing interview in 1999 with John F. Kennedy, Jr., in George Magazine, Mr. Scaife claimed that the Clintons were involved in the deaths of 60 friends and employees—bizarre accusations that have never been taken seriously in a court of law nor been shown to have a basis in fact (Kennedy, 1999).

The Scaife family, however, is not alone in funding the IRD. California-based Fieldstead and Company is the conduit for the interests of Howard Fieldstead Ahmanson, whose father amassed a fortune in the savings-and-loan industry. Howard Ahmanson and his wife, Roberta, who serves on the IRD board of directors, have been key supporters of Chalcedon Inc., the Christian Reconstructionist think tank where Howard Ahmanson served on the board of directors for 23 years (Olsen, 1998). Christian Reconstructionism is a hard-line Calvinist movement that advocates replacing American democracy with a fundamentalist theocracy under strict biblical codes. For example, they would impose the death penalty "by stoning" on everyone from adulterers and homosexuals to incorrigible children and those who spread "false" religions (Robinson, 2002). Ahmanson gave IRD $58,960 in 1991 and $234,135 in 1992 (Howell, 1995) and according to an IRD disclosure recently made to the Washington Post, Ahmanson continues to give on average $75,000 a year (Cooperman, 2003).

Other IRD funding sources include the John M. Olin Foundation, whose namesake manufactured Winchester rifles; Olin has backed the IRD in the amount of $489,000 "to counter the political influence of the Religious Left." The Castle Rock Foundation, created by the Adolph Coors family in 1993, gave $90,000 to IRD to "challenge the orthodoxy promoted by liberal religious leaders in the U.S." The Lynde and Harry Bradley Foundation, funded by a family with ties to the ultra-conservative John Birch Society, gave $1.5 million between 1985 and 2001 to IRD efforts (Media Transparency, 2003). The Bradley

Foundation's stated objective is to return the U.S. to the days before government regulation of business and before corporations were required to negotiate with labor unions (Media Transparency, 2003).

How significant is the relationship between the IRD and this secular-funding base? Between 1985-2002, the IRD ranked 81st in money received on a list of 2609 recipients of funding from right-wing organizations (Media Transparency, 2003). The National Committee for Responsive Philanthropy published a report in 1997 showing how a dozen foundations have prevailed in shaping public policy. It found that the organizations that fund the IRD (and a few others) diverge in their practices from the generally accepted social and ethical norms of the philanthropic sector (National Committee for Responsive Philanthropy, 1997). According to this report, the IRD-supporting foundations' agendas include the aggressive furthering of public policy that favors the wealthy and the use of government power to support corporate interests and laissez-faire capitalism (Media Transparency, 2003).

What does this all mean? At the very least, we can say that the IRD, by uncritically accepting funds from such organizations, tacitly approves their agendas. Conversely, it would appear obvious that the IRD would not receive funding from such groups were it not furthering their objectives.

The IRD's stated goals, which consistently are at odds with the historic social witness of the mainline churches, include increasing military spending, opposing environmental protection efforts and eliminating social welfare programs (Institute on Religion and Democracy, 2001a). In this respect, it can be said that the IRD and its wealthy patrons are intent on derailing if not outright controlling the UMC's social witness. If that sounds implausible, one need only consider how right-wing groups during the last decade have done that and more in their take-over of the Southern Baptist Convention.

How do they operate in pursuit of their goals? The IRD's

modus operandi is to vilify and ridicule UMC officials, organizations and programs that do not reflect its views. For example, in March of 2001, the IRD demonstrated utter contempt for United Methodist bishops in an assault on their collective judgment and integrity; this was published on the Good News Web site under the title, "The Methodist President and His Bishops" (Tooley, 2001a). Mark Tooley, executive director of IRD's United Methodist monitoring program, a former CIA analyst and a board member of Good News, called the bishops en masse "fatuous" and "pompous." According to Mr. Tooley, "statements from United Methodist bishops are often inarticulate and sometimes downright nonsensical." He was particularly agitated by their unanimous vote questioning the proposed expenditure of tens of billions of dollars by the Bush Administration on a "Star Wars" missile defense system that is without proven scientific merit (PBS, 2003). He also was scornful of the bishops when they expressed concern for "children and the poor," who, according to the bishops, are being impoverished as a result of excessive military expenditures (Tooley, 2001a).

The IRD hardly has a good word to say about any United Methodist leaders. For example, when Duke University adopted a policy (supported by both North Carolina bishops) that students and their families could use the university chapel for same-sex blessings by churches that permit them, Mr. Tooley and the IRD unleashed an attack on the Rev. Dr. William Willimon (Willimon, 2001). (Dr. Willimon at the time was Dean of the Chapel at Duke and was elected as a United Methodist bishop in 2004.) When he contacted the IRD to report that he and his secretary were receiving hate mail and pornographic materials in the name of the IRD's protest, Mr. Tooley wrote back saying, "If you can't take the heat, get out of the kitchen." Mr. Tooley stated that he had no interest in talking further with Dr. Willimon until he resigned from Duke (Willimon, 2003).

Dr. Willimon is in good company. IRD has attacked, among others, Archbishop Desmond Tutu, Rev. Jim Wallis of

Sojourners, the evangelical leader Dr. Tony Campolo, the National Council of Catholic Bishops, the UMC's Igniting Ministry public relations campaign (Bowdon, 2001), the UMC's newest hymnal (McIntyre, 2001) and numerous other distinguished Protestant, Catholic, and Jewish leaders and programs (United Methodists Affirming Christ's Teachings in our Nation, 2003; UM Action, 2000).

There's more. For example, when the Interfaith Alliance was formed during the 1990s as a progressive multi-faith group to counter the bullying of the Christian Coalition and others on the religious right, Mr. Tooley took exception. He was upset that prominent and respected Americans like Walter Cronkite were trying to help the multi-faith group (Neuhaus, 1997). Perhaps harking back to his cold-warrior days in the CIA, Mr. Tooley likened several Christian and Jewish leaders to communist stooges: "The Interfaith Alliance's board is about as diverse as a Soviet politburo during the empire's final, geriatric years. Yes, some were bald, others had bushy eyebrows. Some came from Leningrad, others from Minsk. Some were septuagenarians, others were octogenarians and there are two Catholic bishops from the church's left-fringe. Three liberal rabbis. And several Black denominational leaders who shun the social conservatism typical of most black churches" (Neuhaus, 1997).

Of course, he is belittling some of the most eminent religious leaders in America who serve on the Interfaith Alliance Board, including Rabbi David Gelfand, Senior Rabbi at The Jewish Center of the Hamptons in East Hampton, New York; Rev. Gardner C. Taylor, Pastor Emeritus of the Concord Baptist Church of Christ in Brooklyn, and past president of the Progressive National Baptist Convention; and Dr. J. Philip Wogaman, former Dean of Wesley Seminary in Washington, D.C. and retired Senior Minister of Foundry UMC in the nation's capitol (The Interfaith Alliance, 2003).

Mr. Tooley is not alone, however. Diane Knippers, formerly a United Methodist, is now a member of the Truro Episcopal

Church in Fairfax, Virginia and heads up the IRD. Ms. Knippers recently made the claim in The United Methodist Reporter that "The fact is that the IRD rarely takes any kind of political position" (Smith, 2002). Nothing could be farther from the truth. It would be difficult to find a right-wing Republican position that IRD has not rallied behind with gusto. We documented several dozen examples. Following are only a few.

The IRD has pressed the Bush administration to take a harder line on North Korea (Goodenough, 2003) and vigorously supported Republican tax cuts for the rich (Tooley, 2001b, c). Mr. Tooley's direct board of directors supervisor, David Stanley, is the chairman of a radical anti-tax group (Clark, 1999) that advocates the slashing of government services for the poor and disabled and huge tax cuts for the wealthy (Neas, 2003). The IRD opposes even limited environmental protection efforts and has collaborated with other like-minded folks to try to roll back protections now in place (Interfaith Coalition for Environmental Stewardship, 2003; Public Eye, 2003; Sider & Ball, 2002; Tooley, 2002). The IRD, particularly Ms. Knippers, has been vocal in opposition to any form of hate crime legislation (Jones, 2000). It has expressed opposition to a land mines treaty (Institute on Religion and Democracy, 2001b) and to women even having knowledge about reproductive choices (Institute on Religion and Democracy, 2001c).

Further illustrating its political stands, when Dr. Richard Land, former teacher at Criswell College in Dallas, and now president of the Southern Baptist Convention's Ethics and Religious Liberty Commission, spoke out in September 2002 for a preemptive war on Iraq, IRD was virtually the only other "religious" group in America that backed the idea (McMullen, 2002). Even Robert McGinnis, vice president of policy for the conservative Family Research Council, in Christianity Today, said that the U.S. would be justified attacking Iraq only if there were irrefutable evidence linking it to terrorism and the production of weapons of mass destruction for imminent use.

Interlocking Boards & Official Spokespersons for IRD/Good News/Confessing Movement, 2004

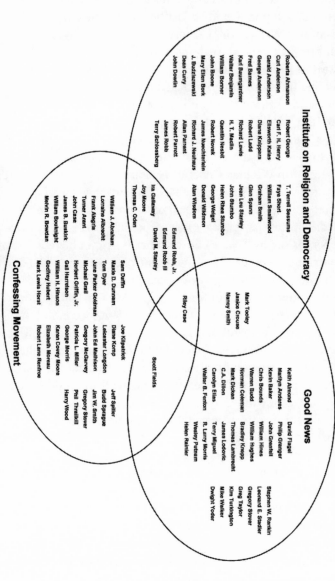

Institute on Religion and Democracy

Roberta Almanson
Curt Anderson
Gerald Anderson
George Anderson
Fred Barnes
Karl Baumgardner
Walter Benjamin
William Bonner
John Boone
Mary Ellen Bork
J. Budziszewski
Dean Curry
John Dowlin

Robert George
Carl F. H. Henry
Ellsworth Kalas
Diane Knippers
Robert Ladd
Richard Lewis
H. T. Maclin
Quentin Nesbit
Robert Novak
James Nuechterlein
Richard J. Neuhaus
Allan Parrent
Robert Parrott
James Robb
Terry Schlossberg

T. Terrell Sessums
Faye Short
William Smallwood
Graham Smith
Glen Spann
Jean Lou Stanley
John Stumbo
Helen Rhea Stumbo
George Weigel
Donald Wildmon
Alan Wisdom

Good News

Keith Almond
Marilyn Anderes
Kevin Baker
Chris Bounds
Warren Budd
Norman Coleman
Mark Dicken
C.A. Dillon
Carolyn Elias
Walter B. Fenton

David Flagel
Philip Granger
John Grenfell
William Hines
Bradley Knepp
Thomas Lambrecht
James Lodovic
R. Larry Morris
Wesley Putnam
Helen Rainier

Stephen W. Rankin
Leonard E. Stadler
Gregory Stover
Greg Taylor
Kim Turkington
Mike Walker
Dwight Yoder

Mark Tooley
Janice Crouse
Nancy Smith

Riley Case

Scott Fields

Joy Moore
Thomas C. Oden

Edmund Robb, Jr.
David M. Stanley

Edmund Robb III

Ira Gallaway

Confessing Movement

William J. Abraham
Lorraine Albrecht
Frank Alegria
Turner Arant
John Case
James B. Buskirk
William Bouknight
Melvin R. Bowdan

Sam Darfin
Maxie D. Dunnam
Tom Dyer
June Parker Goldman
Michael Grall
Herbert Griffin, Jr.
Gail Harrelson
William H. Hinson
Godfrey Hubert
Mark Lewis Horst

Joe Kilpatrick
Diane Komp
Leicester Longdon
John Ed Mathison
Gregory McGarvey
Patricia L. Miller
George Morris
Karen Covey Moore
Elizabeth Moreau
Robert Lane Renfroe

Jeff Spiller
Budd Sprague
Jim W. Smith
Gregory Stover
Phil Thrailkill
Harry Wood

Sources: Websites of all three organizations list Board of Directors for the year. Please see references for web addresses. Created in 2004.

Dr. Land declared in an article released by the Baptist Press that military action would be justified under the ethical standards of Just War Theory because "Saddam Hussein is developing at breakneck speed weapons of mass destruction he plans to use against America and her allies." He stated that, "there is a direct line from those who attacked the U.S. [on Sept. 11] back to the nation of Iraq" (McMullen, 2002).

The IRD "stood tall" with Dr. Land (McMullen, 2002). In the process, Diane Knippers made the statement that comments made by two United Methodist leaders critical of the war on Iraq—Mr. Jim Winkler, General Secretary of the General Board of Church and Society, and the Rev. Bob Edgar, General Secretary of the National Council of Churches-should be disregarded. The Lakeland Ledger newspaper in Florida quoted Ms. Knippers as saying "These church officials cannot be relied upon to contribute intelligently to the debate over war with Iraq, their vision of the world is largely divorced from historic Christian teachings about the use of force . . . "(McMullen, 2002). Our Lord Jesus Christ, whose views toward violence were nothing but disapproving, might consider that an odd point of view! In any event, the Florida newspaper found her opinion reprehensible: "Trying to silence duly elected religious leaders in a matter this momentous is odd indeed for someone who presides over an organization with religion and democracy in its title. Knippers' comments were neither religiously charitable nor democratic. It is difficult to see the views of Land, Knippers, and other like-minded individuals as anything other than a veneer of religious reasoning in the service of an undiluted nationalism" (McMullen, 2002).

Ms. Knippers also supports those who oppose hate crime laws. On August 10,1996, she released a letter in the name of IRD to the media accusing the National Council of Churches (NCC) of "perpetrating a hoax" regarding the well-publicized 1995-1996 African-American church arsons across America (United Methodist News Service, 1996). Ms. Knippers accused the NCC of nefarious conduct, declaring that the 53-year-old ecumenical group had "exaggerated the church burning phenomenon to promote a radical agenda" and that its officials "jawboned" the church burning issue into a national crisis. Ms. Knippers claimed that the NCC had created the church arson story "absent evidence that black churches burn more frequently than white churches to raise money for its leftist political agenda" (United Methodist News Service, 1996).

The NCC responded with facts. It made the point that arson and vandalism at African-American and multi-racial churches had "increased dramatically and persistently over the past 18 to 30 months." The Rev. Joan Brown Campbell, the NCC's chief executive at the time, noted that "more than 60 African-American and multiracial churches were burned between January 1, 1995, and June 30, 1996, more than in the previous five years combined." Dr. Campbell wrote that "while approximately the same number of black and white churches have been burned since 1995, black churches are burning in proportion to their number at four times the rate of white churches" (United Methodist News Service, 1996).

FBI data support the NCC's assertions (Infoplease, 2000). The chief reason for hate crimes is racial bias, with African-Americans at the greatest risk. In 2000, of the 8,063 such crimes reported to the FBI, 54 percent (4,337) were race related, two-thirds of which targeted African-Americans. The types of crimes committed against African-Americans included bombing and vandalizing churches, burning crosses on home lawns, and murder. Among other racially-motivated crimes reported, about 20 percent were committed against European-Americans (Infoplease, 2000).

But Ms. Knippers was undeterred. She expressed bizarre beliefs to the Wall Street Journal on August 9, 1996, charging the NCC with using church-arson "to justify its thesis that America is on the verge of a race war." According to the United Methodist News Service, she went further, claiming that the NCC had misrepresented the church burning issue "to smear... conservative Christians as racists." Hello? Was she suggesting that members of the Ku Klux Klan are merely persecuted conservative Christians?

In some ways, as outrageous as such declarations are, they are consistent with Ms. Knippers' stated convictions in other respects. The IRD has always worked hard for the political agenda of the Right Wing. Ms. Knippers' highly vocal and vigorous opposition to hate-crime laws is just one example (Jones, 2000). She and her staff of eight are all European-American as are the 23 members of the IRD Board of Directors and all 20 members of the UM Action steering committee. Perhaps the IRD's position on hate crimes would be more sensitive if there were a few African-Americans in its organization.

At the same time the IRD is not above using hate language to attack United Methodists and others. Dave Berg, who has identified himself as a "segment producer" for the "Tonight Show with Jay Leno," wrote a commentary for IRD posted on its Web site on May 9, 2003 (Berg, 2003). In this column, after he announced that "the war in Iraq is coming to a victorious close," he attacked "the godless army of America's mainstream Protestant leaders" who "worship at the altar of the United Nations" and "gave aid and comfort" to our enemies. He named Jim Winker, General Secretary of the United Methodist General Board of Church and Society, Bishop Clifton Ives of West Virginia, and Bishop William Dew of Arizona, among his targets. He then directed towards these United Methodist leaders, hateful accusations. He said these respected clergymen have "hatred for President Bush and for America itself" (Berg, 2003).

One aspect of this attack group that merits note is that five of the 23 board members of the IRD are conservative Roman Catholics: Father Richard John Neuhaus, Michael Novak, Robert P. George, George Weigel, and Mary Ellen Bork (wife of Judge Robert Bork). One wonders: What are they doing working on a board and contributing to a group whose central aim is to undermine the witness of Protestant churches (Institute on

Religion and Democracy, 2001a)?

Even after 20 years of bashing, however, there appears to be little grassroots support for IRD within the UMC. In a fundraising letter dated November 5, 1999, signed by Mark Tooley as Executive Director of UM Action and David Stanley as Chairman, they stated "We rely entirely upon the generosity of United Methodists like you. Over 8,000 individual United Methodists are now supporting our ministry, with an average donation of $30" (Stanley & Tooley, 1999). In an October of 2002 interview with the United Methodist Reporter, Mr. Tooley said that "The IRD operates on $1 million annually, about $400,000 of which is from 3,500 donors and goes to UM Action (Smith, 2002). On July 30, 2003, on the IRD Web site, Mr. Tooley said "The annual IRD budget is about $1 million a year, about a third of which goes to our United Methodist program. Half of IRD's budget comes from foundation support, while the other half comes from individual donors. IRD's United Methodist program relies mostly on small donors, of whom we have about 3,000. Their average gift is about $30" (Tooley, 2003).

Using IRD's own numbers, their donor base has dropped from 8000 to 3000, a 62.5 percent loss in less than four years, despite having sent out hundreds of thousands of unsolicited pieces of mail each year. Moreover, Mr. Tooley claims that his annual budget is now about $333,000, half of which he says comes from 3000 donors with an average contribution of $30. The numbers just do not add up!

The truth is that without wealthy right-wing patrons, the IRD would be quickly out of business. Much of the IRD's behavior would simply be dismissed as bad manners by people with poor social skills except that the IRD is well funded by wealthy non-United Methodist backers whose social agendas are at odds with the historical witness of the church. If Scaife, Ahmanson, Olin, Coors, Bradley and their ilk are successful in disrupting the moral leadership of the UMC and other mainline Christian churches, they will have muted America's social conscience and significantly diminished its capacity for responsible civic discourse. At risk is the soul of the church and the nation.

References

Berg, D. (2003). Commentary: Anti-war protestants. Institute on Religion and Democracy. Retrieved on September 30, 2003, from http://www.ird-renew.org/news/news.cfm.

Bowdon, B.A. (2001, Sept. 21) Jesus promises are not pabulum, and they are not baloney! Oklahoma Conference Communications, 4(16). Retrieved on October 14, 2003, from http://www.okumc.org/contact/2001/092101/jesus.html.

Brown, J. (2003). Methodist theologian offers hope for evangelical um churches on property issue. Gospel Caf .Inc. Retrieved on November 24, 2003 from www.gospelcafe.org.

Case, R. (2002). It s time we talk about amiable separation . The New Zion s Herald, 177(6), 21.

Case, R. B. (2003). Do renewal groups threaten the health of United Methodism? Good News Magazine. Retrieved on December 2, 2003, from www.goodnewsmag.org.

Clark, D. G. (1999). Clark opposes proposed Iowa constitutional amendment. Letter published as an op-ed in the Muscatine Journal, June 25, 1999. Retrieved on December 9, 2003, from http://www.muscanet.com/~dclark/published/journal-oped699.html.

Cooperman, A. (2003). Conservatives funding opposition, priest says: Groups insist donors don t set agenda. Washington Post, October 24.

Goodenough, P. (2003, May). Bush urged to reject calls for softer line with North Korea. CNSNews.com. Retrieved from http://www.cnsnews.com/images/ International.gif.

GuideStar, (2002). Institute on Religion & Democracy. Retrieved on December 5, 2003, from www.guidestarbasicinformation.htm.

Hartmann, T. (February 25, 2003). Healthcare reveals real "conservative" agenda - drown democracy in a bathtub. Common dreams center: breaking news & views for the progressive community. Common Dreams. Retrieved on November 20, 2003 from www.commondreams.org.

Henderson, B. (2003). The United Methodist ministerial education

fund. Retrieved on December 2, 2003, from
http://www.NWHillsUMC.org.

Hout, M., Greely, A., & Wilde, M. J. (2001). The demographic impera-
tive in religious change in the United States. American Journal of
Sociology, 107(2), 468-500.

Howell, L. (1995). Funding the war of ideas: A report to the united
church board for homeland ministries. Cleveland, OH: United Church
Board for Homeland Ministries

Howell, L. (2003). *United Methodism @ Risk: A wake up call.*
Kingston, NY: Information Project for United Methodists.

Infoplease. (2000). Summary of hate crime statistics. (2000).
Retrieved March 29, 2002, from
www.infoplease.com/ipa/A0004885.html.

Information Project for United Methodists. (2003). *United
Methodism @ risk: A wake-up call,* by Leon Howell: A story: You ve got
to be kidding. Information Project for United Methodists. Retrieved on
October 14, 2003, from http://www.ipum.org/1marykraus.html.

Institute on Religion and Democracy. (2001a). Institute on religion
and democracy s reforming America s churches project: 2001-2004,
executive summary. Retrieved on September 30, 2003 from www.4reli-
gious-right.info/internal_ document_ird.html.

Institute on Religion and Democracy. (2001b). Church leaders rally
against land mines. Institute on Religion and Democracy. Retrieved on
October 6, 2003, from http://www.ird-renew.org/About/About.cfm.

Institute on Religion and Democracy. (2001c). Methodist agency
endorses reinstatement of funding for overseas abortion. Institute on
Religion and Democracy. Retrieved on October 3, 2003, from
http://www.ird-renew.org/About/About.cfm.

Interfaith Alliance. (2003). Board of Directors. The Interfaith Alliance.
Retrieved on October 3, 2003, from
www.interfaithalliance.org/About/AboutList.cfm.

Interfaith Coalition for Environmental Stewardship. Religion and
the environment. Retrieved on September 26, 2003, from
http://www.stewards.net/About.htm.

Jones, D. (2000). Hate crime petitions gain wide support. Response.
Retrieved on September 30, 2003 from http://gbgm-
umc.org/Response/articles/ hatecrimepets.html.

Kaiser, R.G., & Chinoy, I. (1999). Scaife: Funding father of the right.
Retrieved on September 4, 2003, from www.washingtonpost.com/wp-

srv/politics/special/clinto/stories/scaifemain.

Kennedy, J.F. (1999). Who s afraid of Richard Mellon Scaife? (JFK, Jr. Interviews Richard Mellon Scaife). George Magazine. Retrieved September 4, 2003, from http://www.freerepublic.com/forum/a3693c60d6e04.htm%0DAbridged%20from%20.

McIntyre, D. (2001, Aug. 29). A reply to a letter of concern about the faith we sing. The Faith We Sing. Retrieved on October 14, 2003, from www.gbod.org/worship/events/ faithsing/letterreply.html.

McMullen, C. (2002). Cries of the hawk not silenced: beliefs. Lakeland, FL: Lakeland Ledger Publishing.

Media Transparency. (2003). The money behind the media. Institute on Religion and Democracy, Inc. Retrieved from http://www.media-transparency.org/ search_results/info_on_any_recipient.php?174.

Nation, (2003, December 22). What Recovery? 277(21), 4-5.

National Committee for Responsive Philanthropy. (1997). Conservative foundations prevail in shaping public policies: New report documents public policy impact of 12 core foundations. Retrieved on September 4, 2003, from www.ncrp.org/reports/moving.htm.

National Taxpayers Union. (2003). Upper brackets: The right s tax cut boosters. Retrieved on November 20, 2003 from www.nta.org

Neas, R.G. (2003, March 27). Upper brackets: The right s tax cut boosters. People for the American Way. Retrieved on October 14, 2003, from http://www.pfaw.org/pfaw/general/ default.aspx.

Neuhaus, R.J. (1997, August/September). In the Beauty of Holiness. The Public Square. Retrieved September 26, 2003, from http://www.firstthings.com/ftissues/ ft9708/public.html

Olsen, W. (1998). Invitation to a stoning: Getting cozy with theocrats. Reason. Retrieved on December 1, 2003 from www.reason.com/9811/col.olson.shtml.

PBS. (2003). The strategy: Shield. . . or sword? PBS. Retrieved on December 9, 2003, from www.pbs.org/wgbh.

Public Eye. (1989). Group watch: Institute on Religion and Democracy. Retrieved on September 4, 2003, from http://www.public-eye.org/research/Group_ Watch/Entries-76.htm.

Public Eye. (2003). Environment. The Public Eye. Retrieved from http://www.publiceye.org/magazine/v15n1/State_of_Christian_Rt-09.htm.

Right Wing Organizations (2003). Concerned women for America. Retrieved on November 21, 2003, from www.cwfa.org.

Robinson, B. A. (2002). Christian reconstructionism, dominion theology, and theonomy. Ontario Consultants on Religious Tolerance. Retrieved on November 14, 2003 from www.religioustolerance.org.

Rothmyer, K. (2000). The man behind the mask. Retrieved on September 4, 2003, from Salon, http://www.salon.com/news/1998/04/07news.html.

Sider, R., & Ball, J. (2002). A response to Mark Tooley. Institute on Religion and Democracy. Retrieved on October 2, 2003, from http://www.ird-renew.org.

Smith, S. (2002). New group challenges UMC s right wing. Reporter Interactive. Retrieved September 26, 2003 from http://www.reporterinteractive. org/news/100202/project.htm

Smithson, W.C. (2003). Welcome. Iowa ethics & campaign disclosure board. Retrieved on November 26, 2003, from www.state.ia.us/government/iecdb.

Stanley, D., & Tooley, M. (1999). Letter to United Methodists. United Methodist Action. Retrieved on September 30, 2003, from http://www.ucmpage.org/umaction/ gc200letter.htm

Stone, R.H. (2001). John Wesley s life and ethics. Nashville: Abingdon Press.

Tooley, M. (2001a). A Methodist president and his bishops. Good News. Retrieved on October 3, 2003, from www.goodnewsmag.org/news/bushbish_03_14_01.html.

Tooley, M. (2001b). Church leaders and tax collectors. Institute on Religion and Democracy. Retrieved on October 2, 2003.

Tooley, M. (2001c). Tax cuts statement 1: When your church opposes tax cuts, does it speak for you? Methodist Laity Reform Movement, Institute on Religion and Democracy. Retrieved on October 2, 2003 from http://www.mreform.org/taxcuts_statement_1htm=ird++%22mark++tooley

Tooley, M. (2002). What would Jesus drive? Institute on Religion and Democracy. Retrieved on October 2, 2003, http://www.ird-renew.org.

Tooley, M. (2003, July 30). What is the fight really about? Institute on Religion and Democracy. Retrieved on October 6, 2003, from http://www.ird-renew.org/ About/About.cfm.

Tooley, M. (2003). Report to UM Action board of directors. UM Action News. Retrieved on December 2, 2003, from www.ird.org.

UM Action. (2000). 2000 news reports: UM action briefing. Institute for Religion and Democracy. Retrieved on October 8, 2003, from http://www.ucmpage.org/umaction/ news00.htm.

21

UMAction. (2003). Reform agenda: A reform agenda for United Methodists. The Institute on Religion and Democracy. Retrieved on December 1, 2003, from www.ird.org.

United Methodist News Service. (1996). NCC Responds to IRD. Worldwide Faith News. Retrieved on October 2, 2003, from http://www.wfn.org/1996/08/msg00041.html.

United Methodists Affirming Christ s Teachings in our Nation (2003). Links to the writings of Mark Tooley. United Methodists Affirming Christ s Teachings   in our Nation. Retrieved on October 8, 2003, from http://umaction.org/index.htm.

Willimon, W. (2001). Under fire. Christian Century. Retrieved on October 3, 2003, from http://www.christiancentury.org.

Willimon, W. (2003). Personal Communication, September 14, 2003.

Yepsen, D. (May 4, 2003). Yepsen: Give all our grandchildren a brighter future - in Iowa. Des Moines Register. Retrieved on November 20, 2003 from www.desmoinesregester.com

Zion s Herald (2003) The rich grow richer. Zion Herald,177(6), 22.

ADDENDUM

Who Speaks for the IRD?
Some Representative Voices

David M. Stanley is a 75-year-old patron of UMC renewal groups. He serves on the board of directors of The Confessing Movement and is chairman of IRD's UMAction board of directors (direct supervisor to Mark Tooley). His spouse, Jean Leu Stanley, also is a member of the UMAction steering committee. He is chairman of Pearl Mutual Funds and an attorney. His Iowa law firm Stanley, Lande & Hunter claims several high-profile corporate clients including: General Motors, H.J. Heinz, Monsanto, The Travelers Group, and Texaco. He is co-founder of Iowans for Tax Relief which has a political action committee (PAC) known as Taxpayers United (Yepsen, 2003). Since its inception in December of 1983, Taxpayers United PAC has consistently been one of Iowa's largest PACs. It raised a total of $1,905,598 between 1983 and 2002. Although it claims to be nonpartisan in its statement of purpose, at least 97 percent of its money has gone to Republican legislative candidates (Smithson, 2003).

Mr. Stanley has also been chair of the "granddaddy" of radical anti-tax groups for many years, the National Taxpayers Union (NTU). His spouse also serves with him on the NTU board. Right-wing foundations that help fund NTU include those that fund IRD: Scaife, John M. Olin and others (Neas, 2003). The leading advocate for the Bush administration's massive tax-cuts for the richest Americans is **Grover Norquist** who was NTU's Executive Director before being tapped by Ronald Reagan's White House to head Americans for Tax Reform (National Taxpayers Union, 2003). Mr. Norquist told National Public Radio's Mara Liasson in a May 25, 2001 interview, "I don't want to abolish government. I simply want to reduce it to the size where I can drag it into the bathroom and drown it in the bathtub" (Hartmann, 2003).

According to a recent report from the Congressional Budget Office, Mr. Stanley and Mr. Norquist have been very successful in their efforts to be reverse Robin Hoods. Data shows that the gap between the rich and poor more than doubled from 1979 to 2000. The top one percent of American taxpayers had $862,700 each after taxes, on average in 2000, more than triple the $286,300 they had, adjusted for inflation, in 1979 while the bottom 40 percent in 2000 had $21,118 each, up 13 percent from their $18,695 average in 1979 (Zion's Herald, 2003).

Recent tax cuts by the Bush administration, vigorously promoted by Mr. Stanley and IRD, are rapidly increasing the gulf between the haves and have-nots (Tooley, 2001 b, c). Both Mr. Tooley and Ms. Knippers have made statements in favor of the Bush tax cuts and have chided UMC leaders, including its bishops, who have pointed out the stark imbalance in the tax cuts and their dire effects on the poor (Tooley, 2001 b, c). The IRD has never disclosed its close relationship to David M. Stanley and his activities in the anti-tax movement. This conflict of interest is a breach of ethical conduct by IRD which purports to be a spiritual renewal group, not a political action group.

From a Christian point of view the problem with all of these activities is that the Bible says God is not neutral about the "widows and orphans." The Bible takes sides against the greedy and in favor of the needy (see Psalm 14:4-6; Psalm 113:5-7; Psalm 146:5-9. Psalm 35:10; Psalm 68:5-6; I Samuel 2:8; Malachi 3:5; James 1:27). Callousness towards the poor is not new in Christian history. John Wesley attacked greed in the 18th century noting, that "Christians have ignored the Biblical mandates of piling up wealth such that, 'It might as well be still hid in its original Greek for any notice they take of it.'" (Stone, 2001).

Janice Shaw Crouse is a member of the board of directors of

Good News and on IRD's UMAction steering committee, directing the activities of Mark Tooley. She has been a staff writer for Beverly LaHaye and has assisted Good News in writing petitions for annual conferences (Howell, 2003). Beverly LaHaye's group, Concerned Women for America (CWA), identifies feminism as "anti-god, anti-family." CWA has also been active in the fight against using Harry Potter books in schools (Right Wing Organizations, 2003). Its publications, such as "Harry Potter: Seduction of the Occult," claim that the Harry Potter books promote the practice of witchcraft among children. Beverly LaHaye and her husband Tim are strong supporters of the Rev. Jerry Falwell. In 2001 they gave $4.5 million to Mr. Falwell's Liberty University, where Beverly LaHaye was named a trustee (Right Wing Organizations, 2003). Janice Crouse recently declared, "Certain statements in The Book of Discipline of the United Methodist Church, 2000, are contrary to Bible teachings and need to be revised" (Howell, 2003).

Thomas C. Oden is a member of the board of directors of the Confessing Movement and the Chair of IRD. He is Professor of Theology and Ethics at Drew University. He convened the confessing theologians group that prepared a statement for the October 2002 Association for Church Renewal meeting in Indianapolis. Dr. Oden published a book of essays in 2002 called *A Return to Orthodoxy*. In reviewing Dr. Oden's book, Jeffrey Gros of the U.S. Conference of Catholic Bishops, said it is permeated by "disillusionment, anger and even sarcasm." Gros says "when Oden addresses individuals and institutions with which he disagrees, the book falls far short of the facts and of the Christian fairness that is the scholar's calling." (Howell, 2003).

Dr. Oden is the leading advocate for the use of the "nuclear option" by the "renewal groups" in their perceived culture wars with fellow United Methodists (Brown, 2003). Oden, in a document titled "The Trust Clause Governing Use Of Property In The United Methodist Church," argues that the "True

25

Methodists" need to challenge the Trust Clause to claim United Methodist assets. His 16,500 word protestation, which argues that he and his cohorts in the renewal groups have the only correct theological formulations and therefore should lay claim to their property, can be found on both the Good News (www.goodnewsmag.org/) and UMC Confessing Movement (www.confessingumc.org/) Web sites.

The Fall 2000 official newsletter of the Confessing Movement published a wistful summary of the "nuclear option" written by the Rev. Phil Thrailkill, an official spokesperson for the Movement and pastor of Duncan Memorial United Methodist Church in Georgetown, South Carolina:

One day a judge in a Federal courtroom will read our history and that of our opponents, and the issue will be, Who are the true Methodists? Who is it that has maintained basic continuity with the heritage and who has departed? Who gets the property and the name and the legacy of the tradition? If and when that day comes in a public challenge to the Trust Clause, it will be important that we show ourselves to be the rightful heirs, which we are.

Apparently, some of our United Methodist brothers and sisters in Christ have moved from "If your heart is as my heart, give me your hand" (Wesley, 1747) to "If you do not think as I think give me your land."

Riley Case is a retired member of the North Indiana Conference of The United Methodist Church. He is on IRD's UMAction advisory board, a member of the board of directors of Good News and a contributing editor for Good News magazine, and assistant executive director of the Confessing Movement, as well as a regular contributor to its newsletter and a designated official spokesperson.

Mr. Case openly advocates for schism in The United Methodist Church (Case, 2002). He views the church as being dominated by "a ruling elite" that "taxes the local church and then distributes the funds by political and ideological intrigue."

Among the intrigues he sees is the Ministerial Education Fund (MEF), which was established by the 1968 General Conference in an effort to meet the need for the recruitment and education of persons for ordained ministry. The fund now supports programs for theological education in United Methodist seminaries, scholarship assistance to United Methodist candidates for ordained ministry, the Course of Study to train Local Pastors, continuing education, and other programs critical for the development of clergy for local churches.

The MEF is distributed though a covenant formula by which 25 percent is retained in annual conferences for their programs of education and professional support, while the remaining 75 percent is given to the General Board of Higher Education and Ministry, three-fourths of which is used to directly support our 13 United Methodist theological schools. The Discipline of The United Methodist Church requires that every dollar be spent on the current educational expenses of students (Henderson, 2003).

Mr. Case and the IRD (UMAction, 2003) are seeking to move the MEF toward a voucher system, administered by individual annual conferences, that would divert United Methodist dollars from the denomination's schools of theology to independent theological seminaries and other denomination's institutions. The Association of United Methodist Theological Seminaries opposes the proposed "voucher" system for many reasons, most importantly because it would hurt United Methodist seminaries and their United Methodist students. Schools with smaller endowments count on the MEF for their very existence. For example, 80 percent of the budget of the UMC's only predominately African-American theology school, Gammon Theological Seminary, comes from the MEF. Mr. Case's proposal would effectively destroy Gammon.

Mr. Case and the IRD (Institute on Religion and Democracy, 2001a; UM Action, 2000; Tooley, 2003) repeatedly use the "Big Lie" propaganda method to justify their assault on the UMC. It goes like this: The decline in membership in the UMC and other mainline churches is the fault of "liberals" who got the church involved in social action. Mr. Case recently wrote in the Good News magazine that United Methodism "is in the midst of a 100-year decline. The years of the decline correspond exactly to the years that liberalism and institutionalism have dominated Methodism" (Case, 2003).

Mr. Case makes a fundamental error in logic. Correlation does not equate with causation. For example, there is probably a direct correlation between increased consumption of ice cream in Alaska and higher numbers of bank robberies. However, one would not try, hopefully, to suggest that eating more ice cream causes increased criminal behavior. The causal link is the weather. Warmer temperatures in the summer in Alaska produce more ice cream consumption as well as more outdoor activities, including bank robbing.

Demographic research shows that the reason for the decline in membership in mainline churches and the growth of conservative churches like the Southern Baptist Convention, the Assemblies of God and smaller Pentecostal and Holiness churches has little to do with ideology and much to do with biology. Conservative church members have more children. According to several leading experts in the sociology of religion who published their scientific findings in the American Journal of Sociology:

A combination of higher birth rates and earlier childbearing among conservative women . . . explains over three-fourths of the observed change in Protestants' denominational affiliations for cohorts born between 1900 and 1970. Most of the rest of the observed change is caused by falling rates of switching from conservative to mainline denominations; differential apostasy plays a small but significant role. Remarkably, because it has not increased over the past 50 years or so, switching from mainline to conservative denominations as the focus of the leading explanations explains none of the decline of mainline denominations (Hout, Greely & Wilde, 2001*)*.

28

Response to "Follow the Money": An Interview with Mark Tooley

STEPHEN SWECKER

Mark D. Tooley is executive director of UM Action, a program division of the Institute on Religion and Democracy. The following interview was conducted by the editor of Zion's Herald magazine, Stephen Swecker.

ZH – You've seen the Weaver/Seibert article. What do you think?

MT - Well, I thought it was a polemical piece. I thought some of the facts were questionable. They seem to rely heavily on secondary sources when referring to our statements, and that has led to some mischaracterization of things we've said and done in the past.

ZH – Can you give some specifics?

MT - One thing that comes to mind is the response from Will Willimon when we publicized his approval of same-sex unions at the Duke University Chapel. The article claims that I told Dr. Willimon I wouldn't talk to him until he resigned, which is not true. It also quotes me saying that, "If you can't stand the heat you'd better get out of the kitchen," referring to the correspondence that Dr. Willimon received from people who disagreed with his policy. That's how Dr. Willimon characterized his impression of what I said in an article he wrote for Christian Century. What I, in fact, told Dr. Willimon was that I was sorry he got the hateful correspondence, but that I also received hateful letters and that it was an unfortunate part of what can be expected when you're a public figure and make controversial statements in public.

ZH – Is there anything else that you challenge on factual grounds?

MT – Regarding church arsons, the insurance industry at the time (1995-96) estimated that about 500 churches suffer arson every year. About one-fifth of U.S. churches are estimated to be predominantly black. For black churches to have been suffering disproportionately, as the National Council of Churches maintained, it would need to have shown that more than 100 black churches were suffering arson per year, which neither the NCC nor any other group ever showed. The article states that the FBI supported the NCC's assertions, but cites no relevant data. When IRD President Diane Knippers was referring to the church arson story being used to "smear" conservative Christians, she was not referring to the KKK, as the article implies. She was referring to quotes from church leaders at National Council of Churches events linking church arsons to the 1994 elections, to political activism by the Christian Coalition, and so on.

ZH – The article refers to the financial support base for IRD and says the numbers don't add up. An implication is that the support base for IRD is shrinking.

MT - There again, I think it simply is a misunderstanding. To my knowledge, over the nine years I've worked here the number of United Methodist donations has basically been stable. When I started in 1994, we had about 200 Methodist donors and now the number fluctuates between 3,000 and 5,000, although at one point I believe the article said we had something approaching 8,000. I'm also quoted in the article as saying that the average gift from a Methodist donor is about $30 and the authors say the numbers don't add up. But I think they misunderstood. When we say $30, the donor will give us a gift several times a year of $30, not simply a total of $30 for the year. The average individual gift is $30, and then the donor contributes several times a year.

ZH – What's the focus of your work?
MT - Well, my individual work is reform of the United Methodist denomination. For IRD overall, it has been from the beginning over 20 years ago religious liberty, spotlighting the plight of persecuted Christians around the world, encouraging U.S. churches to be more outspoken on their behalf and encouraging accountability within the structures of the denominations. One of the chief problems regarding the lack of accountability in the UMC is that the average church member knows nothing about what is going on beyond his or her local congregation. My calling is to make sure the average United Methodist is aware of what's happening in the national church.

ZH - I'm surprised to hear you say there's a lack of accountability. The UMC is governed through an electoral process, and boards and agencies are overseen by elected boards of directors.
MT - One example of what I'm referring to is the Board of Church and Society, which functions more as a caucus group than an agency representing the whole church. We think that agency largely ignores the theological convictions of most United Methodists and devotes its energy to controversial issues that divide the church rather than unify it.

ZH - Are you implying that Church and Society is out of step with the church's *Book of Discipline*?
MT - On some issues they definitely are, and the obvious example would be homosexuality which the church has debated for 30 years and keeps coming to the same conclusion. But Church

31

and Society continues to dissent and to show how very different its board members are from the rest of the church.

ZH – Your response suggests the IRD views the *Discipline* as carved in stone.

MT - The *Book of Discipline* is not revealed truth, obviously. It's a book of law for one denomination that can be changed every four years. But in between those four years it is important that the church uphold what is in the *Discipline.*

ZH - What do you say to the argument that each generation has a responsibility to wrestle with its tradition in light of its own experience?

MT – Obviously, each generation needs to struggle with its faith and to define its faith, but I think that each generation of Christians is called to be faithful to the previous generation of Christians and not be mindful only of its own experience. There are some teachings that perhaps are malleable and tend to be shifted with the times, but beneath that there is a foundation that I believe is constant.

ZH – Who has the authority to define that "constant foundation"?

MT - Well, we as Protestants believe the Scriptures themselves are the final authority for everything we say about God and salvation. The tradition of the last 200 years is also an important tool in understanding what the Scriptures are saying to us.

ZH – Where does the IRD get its authority to make judgments about that tradition or the Scriptures?

MT - We don't claim any specific authority other than the fact that we are primarily lay people in mainline churches who want fellow members of our churches to be better informed and more involved in the governing of the church. So, 80-90 percent of what we do is not advocacy but simply putting out information that generally is not available in official church media.

ZH - The article states that although the IRD says it doesn't take political positions, it in fact does.

MT - I think that's a common misunderstanding, that when we critique or disagree with the political stances taken by the lobbying offices of the denominations or of their bishops or other church leaders, that we are endorsing a contrary position or encouraging a church to endorse a contrary position. In fact, that's not the case. We did not endorse the war in Iraq, for example. In fact, I thought that was another mischaracterization in the article.

ZH - But you have chastized church leaders who have, in fact, taken positions against the war, for example, and you say that should not be construed as taking a political position yourself?

MT - That's right. When the article suggests that we endorsed the war along with Richard Land and the Southern Baptist convention, that's simply not the case. In fact, Diane Knippers was asked to sign a letter drafted by Richard Land, and she declined to do so.

ZH - But you have made derogatory statements about church leaders who took a position *against* the war.

MT - That's right. But basically, we questioned whether the institutional church should permit its clergy, its agencies, in the name of the church, to be routinely used to endorse specific political policies.

ZH - So you wouldn't subscribe to the adage that politics is too important to be left to the politicians?

MT - I don't think the specifics of politics are the vocations of bishops or clergy or full-time church employees. I think it's the calling or vocation of Christian lay people.

ZH - One could read into what you just said that IRD places a great deal of faith in government itself and that it has a bias toward the judgment of political leaders as opposed to church leaders.

MT - No, I would say just the opposite. I would say Christianity understands human sinfulness and should be skeptical about all structures and powers, including government or any bureaucracy, which could include church structures. So I hope good citizens and good Christians will challenge all governance. Once again, I don't think that's the vocation of the leadership of the institutional church. The leadership of the institutional church, by proclaiming the Gospel, presumably will inspire church members to take very seriously their role as citizens.

ZH - Who in the world is empowered to critique government if it's not those whose lives are given professionally and vocationally to grappling with the practical implications of Christian teaching?

MT - I think the temptation to take political stances was one that Christ specifically avoided, as did the apostles and, by-and-large, John Wesley. I commend their examples to the leaders of today's institutional church.

ZH - There are some critics of the IRD who, in so many words, think of the IRD and Mark Tooley as the devil incarnate. How do you respond to such harsh characterizations?

MT - Well, I think that there is great frustration among church elites about the criticism they receive and their lack of widespread support. They have developed an explanation for their frustration that falls upon particular groups, specifically, the more conservative or evangelical renewal groups within the church. But I would respond that we who are in the evangelical renewal groups would ourselves be powerless if it were not for the fact that many, many United Methodists share our perspective.

ZH - Anything else you'd like to comment on?

MT – I think that the Weaver/Seibert article, like the *United Methodism @ Risk* book, was primarily an expression of frustration over what they fear is the declining influence of liberal theology and a liberal political perspective within The United Methodist Church. I think there's good cause for them to be concerned, in that demographically the liberal parts of Methodism don't seem to have a very bright future. I think that their blaming it primarily or exclusively on the IRD or other renewal groups is not fair or accurate. Trends that are taking place in Methodism are taking place in other mainline denominations and in the Christian church worldwide. The future of Christianity seems to belong to a more historically orthodox perspective.

ZH - So the right-wing funding sources for IRD that the Weaver/Seibert article identifies are getting a good return on their investment, do you think?

MT - Well, the article, the *@ Risk* book and other liberal critics of IRD have expressed great concern about conservative foundations funding IRD, but it should not be shocking that conservative groups receive their support from conservative individuals and conservative foundations. The foundations that the article describes and portrays as being extreme or hyper right-wing are involved in mainstream political activity. It's fine to disagree with that perspective, but it's unfair or inaccurate to portray it as extreme or outside the mainstream.

Embedded: Charting
the IRD's Ties to the Radical Right

NICOLE SEIBERT & ANDREW J. WEAVER

I n the January/February 2004 issue of Zion's Herald, we published a special report on the activities of the Institute on Religion and Democracy (IRD). We documented how the IRD is primarily funded by right-wing secular foundations with an ultra-conservative political agenda. We also showed the interlocking relationships between IRD and two other conservative, self-styled "renewal" groups in the United Methodist Church (UMC), Good News and the Confessing Movement. And we explained that IRD is used as a hammer against the UMC by the Confessing Movement and Good News which both publish IRD's ridicule, distortions and falsehoods regarding UMC leaders and programs (Howell, 2003). Its strategy is designed to de-legitimize church leadership in the eyes of members and cause schism in the church.

The IRD answers only to its own self-perpetuating board of directors, most of whose members are embedded in the secular radical right (see chart above). IRD directors are on the boards

Media Social Networks of IRD Board Members

The 2004 Board of Directors of IRD have editorships, repeated publications or are on the Boards of Directors of these media outlets.

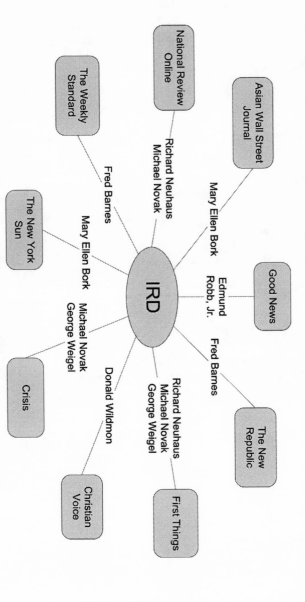

National Review Online

The Weekly Standard

Asian Wall Street Journal

The New York Sun

Richard Neuhaus
Michael Novak

Fred Barnes

Mary Ellen Bork

Mary Ellen Bork

IRD

Edmund Robb, Jr.

Fred Barnes

Good News

Michael Novak
George Weigel

Donald Wildmon

Richard Neuhaus
Michael Novak
George Weigel

The New Republic

Crisis

Christian Voice

First Things

Sources: Institute on Religion and Democracy website and Right Web, http://rightweb.irc-online.org/index.php, accessed 2004.

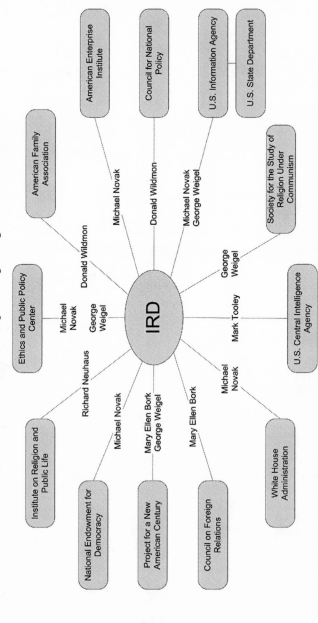

Social Network Ties of Select IRD Board Members
Focus on Government and Religious Right Organizations, 2004

Sources: Institute on Religion and Democracy website and Right Web, http://rightweb.irc-online.org/index.php, accessed 2004.

and actively involved in right-wing groups such as the Project for the New American Century, Institute on Religion and Public Life, National Taxpayers Union, Concerned Women for America, Ethics and Public Policy Center, and American Enterprise Institute. IRD board members operate and have access to conservative publications and media such as First Things, Good News, Christianity Today, Washington Times, The Weekly Standard and Fox News.

The IRD also has the same group of benefactors that regularly contribute to ultra-right causes such as the Lynde and Harry Bradley Foundation, the Smith Richardson Foundation, the John M. Olin Foundation, the California billionaire Howard Ahmanson and the Sarah Scaife Foundation (Blumenthal, 2004; Howell, 2003). As was reported recently in the New York Times, "The mainline denominations are a strategic piece on the chess board that the right wing is trying to dominate" (Goodstein and Kirkpatrick, 2004).

References

Blumenthal, M. (2004). Avenging angel of the religious right. Retrieved on January 6, 2004; http://archive.salon.com/news/feature/2004/01/06/ahmanson/index.html.

Goodstein, L. and Kirkpatrick, D.D. (2004) Conservative Group Amplifies Voice of Protestant Orthodoxy, New York Times, Retrieved May 22, 2004.
http://query.nytimes.com/gst/abstract.html?res=F0071FFA345B0C718E DDAC0894DC404482

Howell, L. (2003). United Methodism @ Risk: A wake up call. Kingston, NY: Information Project for United Methodists.

Weaver, A. J. and Seibert, N. (2004) Secular conservative philanthropies waging unethical campaign to take over United Methodist Church. Mediatransparency.org , August 2, 2004. http://www.mediatransparency.org/stories/irdi.html

Purveyors of False Memory: Unmasking the Institute on Religion and Democracy

THOM WHITE WOLF FASSETT

On November 18, 1995 at 10:29 a.m., I stood in the White House Oval Office with my hand on the back of the President of the United States as one of a small group of religious leaders encircling him in prayer. Within the week, a Washington-based group called the Institute on Religion and Democracy (IRD) attacked us for praying with the president.

Since its inception in the earlier 1980s, the IRD has attacked mainline denominations as they sought to fulfill the mandates of their respective governing bodies, all the while proclaiming, however, that "religious freedom is the cornerstone of human rights and democracy." Hence, this particular Nov. 18 attack on religious freedom was a surprising new strategy. It left us more deeply convinced that political, not religious, motives drove the staff and supporters of IRD. The real offense eliciting the attack that day was the fact that religious leaders were asking the president to veto a welfare bill that would remove the social safety

40

net for untold numbers of women and children. This was not politically acceptable to the IRD.

Having spent nearly 20 years in Washington, D.C., as a staff person with the social action agency of The United Methodist Church, I was no stranger to the goals and activities of the IRD. As the agency's chief executive for more than 12 years, I became intimately acquainted with the organization as its leaders launched assaults on me personally and on The United Methodist Church routinely. Nothing but a complete takeover of the church seemed to be their objective.

We now know that the IRD's takeover agenda includes not only The United Methodist Church but the Episcopal Church and the Presbyterian Church (USA) as well. This is made clear, for example, in a privately-circulated 14-page IRD document titled, "Reforming America's Churches Project, 2001-2004."

In the document, which is written as a funding proposal, IRD officials claim that liberal theology has failed the mainline churches, resulting in the loss of millions of members. During 2001-2004, they claim there will be "rare opportunity to redirect these churches away from their reflexive alliance with the political left and back towards classical Christianity." The paper is replete with discussions of "the right" and "the left" and political language that polarizes people across the spectrum of religious conviction. Declaring that they will spend more than $3.6 million over the next four years to promote their agenda, they anticipate contributions from United Methodists of at least $500,000.

This is nothing new. During its 20 years of existence, the IRD has not changed its goals. Founded in 1981 by political activists and evangelical religious leaders, the organization was formed to investigate and oppose certain social action programs of the mainline Protestant churches and became absorbed in tracking the social action funds managed by the denominations. The founding document of the IRD was a report on the funding of outside groups by The United Methodist Church written by

41

David Jessup, at that time a new member of The United Methodist Church living in Silver Spring, Maryland.

Jessup's report, "Preliminary Inquiry Regarding the Financial Contributions to Outside Political Groups by Board and Agencies of The United Methodist Church (UMC), 1977-1979," became the basis of debate and ongoing inquiry within the church concerning its social action expenditures. Although, according to available records, the document was shared with a few delegates attending the General Conference of 1980, no legislative action was taken at that time. Significantly, however, the Good News Forum, an evangelical caucus within the UMC, supported the Jessup document because it reflected their ongoing concerns over a number of years.

In those early days, the board membership of IRD was dominated by well-known intellectuals such as sociologist Peter Berger and authors Richard John Neuhaus and Michael Novak. The board membership was variously associated with the Coalition for a Democratic Majority, the American Enterprise Institute, Social Democrats, U.S.A., and other groups interested in combating communism.

These high-profile board members eventually abandoned the IRD, ostensibly because it turned out not to be the vehicle they had anticipated for their political ambitions. Others remained for a time: David Jessup, Paul Morell, Virginia Law Shell, Ira Gallaway and, notably, Ed Robb of the Robb Evangelistic Association, who galvanized the relationship between Good News and IRD and now, by implication, other UMC church-related "renewal" movements. This would include "Renew," the women's organization now attacking United Methodist Women across the nation.

Ed Robb's son, James, staffed the IRD offices for a period of time. It is important to note that Good News magazine has, from the beginning of IRD, carried sympathetic articles and harsh critiques of the official structures of the UMC, much in keeping with the political objectives of IRD. At that time in the

IRD's early days, two graduate students hired by United Methodist and United Church of Christ agencies concluded in their research on the IRD that its board was composed of two groups, the Social Democrats/USA and its associates, and the leaders of Good News.

IRD funding patterns continue today as they have from the beginning with contributions from individuals, evangelical groups and foundations such as the Smith Richardson Foundation and the Pittsburgh-based foundation of Richard Mellon Scaife. Whatever success the IRD achieves in implementing its programs today is based primarily on the co-option of faith-based organizations to realize its political goals.

Its leaders serve, for example, rather like "recovered memory" therapists who tell United Methodists that their church has taken ridiculous and abhorrent positions on the most critical issues facing humankind today. Hearing this, members who typically do not have their church's teachings in front of them to refute the allegations, react strongly and negatively only to learn afterwards that they are victims of "false memory syndrome." That is, they have been the pawns in a very unethical game of dissembling, obfuscation and outright lies by a secular political organization that more closely resembles a religious caucus of the right wing of the Republican Party.

I belong to no political party. Rather, I write as a United Methodist Christian and out of a context of extensive experience in the church. In previous years and during my term as chief executive of the General Board of Church and Society (now a target for elimination by IRD), I had invited IRD officials to participate with religious leaders and denominational coalitions in Washington to work together toward common goals; these related to various advocacies and national legislation projects designed to implement the Social Principles of The United Methodist Church and the mandates of the General Conference. However, they have refused to share in any work of the UMC but continue to conduct pamphleteering and media strategies opposing most moral and ethical imperatives articulated by the church's governing body. Likewise, over the years, I extended invitations to the Good News Forum to dialogue with the General Board of Church and Society around critical issues of mutual concern facing the church. Good News never responded to the invitations.

Embedded in the IRD is the United Methodist Action Committee which church members often mistake as an official organization of The United Methodist Church. Along with the IRD itself, it is a privately funded, self-appointed, secular lobbying group that attacks the Bible-based, prophetic efforts authorized by the General Conference. They stand in sharp contrast to the church's social action agency; the General Board of Church and Society, for example, has over 60 elected members from the denomination who are engaged in ministries officially mandated and paid for by the church (see particularly paragraphs 1002 and 1004 of the 2000 *Book of Discipline*). These directives are firmly planted in the historic constitution and the doctrinal statements of the church.

The IRD has, to its credit, cultivated powerful media spokespersons to extend their agenda. Brit Hume of Fox Television and syndicated columnist Cal Thomas are but two examples of media celebrities who frequently and uncritically pass on to the American public political analyses produced by the IRD without checking their sources or the veracity of their findings. These relationships have ill served both the UMC constituency and the secular public by promoting IRD's questionable political views as though they were verifiable researched issues related to mainline religious organizations.

For instance, the General Board of Church and Society shipped nearly 500 donated computers to Cuba for Christian brothers and sisters to form a healthcare network; the purpose was to track aspirin, antibiotics, and other medicines to help save the lives of people. This shipment was achieved through tedious negotiations with the United States and the legal transport of these computers to Cuba with the assistance of the government of the United States. The IRD charged us, however, with shipping these computers to "communist Cuba, despite the US embargo."

The IRD mantra appropriately includes attacks on totalitarian states and the lack of the free exercise of religion. But its officials took no notice upon my return from Cuba, having negotiated for seven hours personally with Fidel Castro around principles of religious practice in Cuba. Little notice is given to the fact that Methodist and Presbyterian churches are the fastest growing churches in Cuba, in some part the result of our ecumenical lobbying of the Castro government to loosen restraints on religious practice.

Issues of homosexuality and abortion rights have been the bread-and-butter issues for both the IRD and Good News. These two issues have netted them more financial contributions and more members than all of the other issues combined. This has been achieved only by obfuscation and publication of dis-information to the church's constituents.

The policies of The United Methodist Church on these issues, however, are clear and straightforward. Anyone actually reading them could not possibly misinterpret them. So rampant are the misinterpretations of these issues by IRD, however, and so effective are they in broadly communicating their misinterpretation that they have opened a rift in the family of faith that will not soon be healed. There are, of course, legitimate differences in the family of faith related to these issues, and they will continue to be adjudicated by the general church in the General Conference, which is the only body that can speak for the UMC.

The focus in the IRD's above-mentioned campaign to reform America's churches includes marriage initiatives, overseas religious persecution, environmentalism, national security, hate crimes, federal social entitlements, and church-state conflicts. Through these issues, IRD presents a partisan political platform that:

• demeans women as heads of households and poor people

needing public assistance while alarming the public by implying that homosexual marriage is a goal of mainline denominations;

• correctly cites the persecution of Sudan's Christian minority while refusing to work with mainline denominations on issues of religious freedom in the U.S. or joining them in blocking trade agreements with China because of human rights violations;

• discredits mainline church advocacies related to global warming because of tax implications and their refusal to acknowledge scientific research;

• insists on increasing national security budgets while falsely implying the loss of national sovereignty by continued participation in the United Nations and other international bodies to peacefully resolve international conflicts;

• fails to acknowledge hate crimes as applying to no other category than crimes against racial and ethnic minorities;

• slashes government entities that guarantee fair treatment for all persons in a democracy and the care of millions who have no medical insurance and children who go hungry every day; and

• touts the free exercise of religion while marrying it to new and emerging forms of Christian nationalism as a patriotic standard.

By contrast with the IRD's polarizing agenda, it is time to dispense with the pathetic extremes of Left and Right, the so-called liberal and conservative definitions denoting an outdated spectrum that simply no longer defines the whole range of options in today's world. Instead, we must embrace what some have called the "transformative alternative," salvation through the witness of Jesus Christ that moves public debate away from obsolete arguments between the Right and the Left and finds liberation in deceptively simple Gospel lessons, uncompromising in their directness and utterly understandable regarding the nature and will of God. This endeavor is not designed for the timid or the faint-hearted. Criticism will come from vested interests that are threatened by it, and they will retaliate with speed and force.

Making individual disciples of Jesus Christ is a rewarding activity. But, notwithstanding the IRD's campaign to reform America's churches, we also must be engaged in sharing authentic biblical Good News through the ministry of corporate salvation. In doing so, we seek liberation and deliverance of the whole person, and, ultimately, a redeemed society which recognizes that:

• working toward harmony and right relations within all of God's creation is Good News;

• feeding the hungry spirit and the hungry body is Good News;

• promoting human dignity and justice for all is Good News;

• relieving those who are oppressed, dehumanized by systems and weighed down by layers of subjugation, is Good News; and

• sharing with humankind the unspeakable love of God is Good News.

References

1. "The Institute on Religion and Democracy s, Reforming America s Churches Project, 2001-2004," p. 4.

2. Ibid., p.1.

3. Ibid.

4. Eric Hochstein and Ronald O Rourke, "A Report on the Institute on Religion and Democracy," Reissued August, 1985, p. i.

5. Ibid.m, p. a, and following.

6 Ibid., p. 18.

Response: Open Churches Welcome Dissent

DIANE KNIPPERS and MARK TOOLEY

Thom White Wolf Fassett wants to have it both ways, or several ways. He wants the United Methodist Church's Board of Church and Society routinely to promote controversial positions on public policy issues. But "secular" groups are not supposed to criticize the board, lest this be seen—inexplicably -as a violation of the board's religious freedom. Members of the church who disagree with the board's policies are to be labeled "secular" by virtue of their organized opposition to official church statements.

Critics of the board are "partisan." But the board's own reliably left-leaning political witness is not. Fassett describes himself as exclusively shaped by Christianity and United Methodism. Presumably, those who disagree with his politics must be infected by other, more worldly impulses.

Fassett portrays opposition within the church to its policies as being almost entirely and artificially created by outside forces with a nefarious secular agenda. What is actually pretty simple

48

Fassett turns into something mysterious and conspiratorial.

Here is the simple part: the Board of Church and Society is a liberal activist church agency that is supposed to represent a denomination, 60 to 70 percent of whose members tell pollsters they are conservative. There is no mystery as to why this leads to dissension.

Imagine, if it's possible, the Washington lobby office of the Unitarian Universalist Association routinely fighting against abortion, for increased military spending, against gun control, and for tax vouchers for private religious schools. Imagine the response from most Unitarians, who are, we presume, comfortably liberal.

Likewise, the majority of United Methodists—who are conservative-leaning, mostly living in the south and midwest, and centered primarily in small towns and suburbs—are not the natural constituency for the brand of politics advocated by Fassett and the Board of Church and Society. It is that gap between church agencies such as the Board of Church and Society or the Women's Division of the Board of Global Ministries that so worries, even threatens, the ideological agenda of agency staff. The Institute on Religion and Democracy is largely the messenger. But, better attempt to discredit the IRD than the people whose tithes and offerings pay the bills.

Our objection to Thom Fassett's Nov. 19, 1995 visit with President Bill Clinton—when a National Council of Churches delegation laid hands on the president and prayed that he would be "strong for the task" of resisting the Republican Congress—was not because we were angry about church people praying with a Democratic president. Democrats presumably need prayers as much as Republicans.

Rather, we thought it highly inappropriate for the leaders of Christian churches to declare unequivocally that the Christian Gospel favors the leader of one political party against the leadership of another political party based on issues over which there are legitimate differences of opinion among believing

Christians. Our proposal was for the church leaders to meet and pray with Republican Congressional leaders as well. (We also thought that putting out press releases about partisan prayers was manipulative and, well, tacky.)

The issue that most exercised those religious leaders, welfare reform, involved a debate over whether responsibility for helping the poor lies primarily with the federal government or with individual state governments. Is there clear biblical teaching on this issue? Fassett and other NCC leaders were confident regarding the Republican budget proposals that "appallingly, in the name of balancing the budget, the moral vision is discarded." But we think most United Methodists would agree the issue is more complicated, and that faithful Christians can disagree. Indeed, we suspect most United Methodists today would conclude that, on balance, welfare reform has been beneficial in moving many families off welfare and toward self-sufficiency.

Fassett writes of IRD's "obfuscation," "disinformation," "dissembling" and "outright lies." The only example he cites is IRD's criticism of his agency's intervention several years ago on behalf of Lucius Walker of Pastors For Peace. Walker's group regularly attempts to ship material illegally to Cuba to discredit what it views as an immoral embargo by the United States. Some of Walker's activists and the computers they were carrying were seized by U.S. Customs officials. Walker was allowed to wage a hunger strike on the grounds of the United Methodist Building in Washington, D.C., which is owned by the agency Fasset directed at the time. Meanwhile, Fassett, among others, helped persuade the U.S. Commerce Department to release most of the computers and ship them to Cuba.

Since Walker openly praises Fidel Castro and denies there are fundamental problems with a one-party communist state, support by Fassett's agency for Walker and his campaign seemed highly inappropriate. Indeed, we have not seen where Fassett or any Church and Society representative has ever publicly expressed criticism of Fidel Castro's government. Once again, the IRD recognizes that Christians may responsibly take different positions regarding the efficacy of the embargo. What we cannot understand is silence in the face of repression.

Fassett provides no other examples of IRD's supposed obfuscations. He claims we misquote from his board's statements and exploit the fact that most church members do not have original church documents. In fact, we are eager to refer our readers and supporters to the church's website so they can examine these statements for themselves.

Not only are most church members oblivious to these statements, but we invariably learn they are oblivious to the very existence of the Board of Church and Society as a lobby agency in the nation's capital—an agency that adopts controversial political stances in the church's name. Usually, they are less than enthusiastic about a church lobby office.

Though unmentioned by Fassett, 30 percent of the delegates to the General Conference of the United Methodist Church voted in 2000 to eliminate the Board of Church and Society altogether. This was remarkable given that the delegates there are far more institutional and less conservative than the average United Methodist.

Is this widespread dissatisfaction with the board totally owing to the "obfuscation" of the IRD? That's an insult to church members who are perfectly capable of making their own judgments.

There are several factual inaccuracies in Fassett's article. In response to the original report on United Methodist grants to outside groups done by David Jessup, an IRD founder, the 1980 General Conference did vote to mandate full disclosure of budgetary information, including grants, by church agencies. Fassett implied that the General Conference ignored Jessup's report.

Fassett said that "intellectuals" and "high profile" board members have since "abandoned" us. In fact, Richard John Neuhaus and Michael Novak, whom he specifically cites, are still on our board. And they have been joined over the years by other leading theologians, scholars, and activists, including J. Budziszewski,

Robert George, Thomas Oden, and others. Indeed, the IRD boasts one of the most prestigious boards of any Christian organization in the nation.

Fassett declares that IRD has a "partisan political platform." As examples, he says we want to "demean women as heads of households and poor people needing public assistance." We are not sure exactly what he means, but perhaps he is referring to our criticism of the mainline churches' one-sided opposition to welfare reform. Or perhaps he disagrees with our publicizing social science data warning of the detrimental effects of father-absence on children, families, and communities of all economic strata.

He decries that we are "alarming" the public by complaining of mainline churches that support same-sex unions. It is well known that many senior leaders in mainline denominations actively support acceptance of homosexual "marriage." This, and not our complaints, is why these denominations are so embroiled in debate over this issue. (It is interesting that the directors of the Board of Church and Society routinely vote overwhelmingly to oppose United Methodist teaching on homosexuality even as those teachings are being solidly reaffirmed by the General Conferences.)

Fassett complains that IRD will not work together with mainline denominations on behalf of persecuted Christians in Sudan. In fact, we have worked closely on this issue with the Episcopal Church's Washington office. We have had trouble persuading other mainline lobby offices, including Fassett's, to take up the issue as a major focus. Fassett wishes we had worked with his agency to block trade agreements with China because of human rights violations. Here's the irony: It was the United Methodist Board of Global Ministries that disagreed with the social action agency, not us. While IRD did not take a position on this, I suspect most of our sympathies were, in fact, with Church and Society.

He bemoans our lack of enthusiasm for "global warming" issues, speaks of our "insisting on increasing national security budgets" (which we have never done to our knowledge), does not like it that we are skeptical about adding "sexual orientation" to hate crimes laws, and alleges that we want to "slash" government agencies that ensure fair treatment for all people and that we are indifferent to people without health insurance. By this, he evidently means we do not wish for churches to back socialized medicine as the only answer to the nation's health care problems.

Fassett is also distressed by the "emerging forms of Christian nationalism as a patriotic standard." We suspect that Fassett has been troubled by Christian leaders who have prayed with the current president, giving him support and strength for the U.S. war against terrorism. We think ultimately Fassett would agree with us that public prayers by church leaders with national leaders have important political implications and are not outside the realm of critique and analysis.

We richly enjoyed Fassett's description of the IRD, especially its founding, as rooted in a hodgepodge of Trotskyites, Social Democrats, Reaganites (as well as those who had worked for Carter's election or who served in the Clinton administration), and Good News evangelicals. (He left out the Episcopal ethicists, pro-life activists, labor organizers, the pope's biographer, a pre-eminent patristics scholar, the founding editor of Christianity Today, and the editor of First Things.) Now that is a vast conspiracy, indeed! No wonder he is worried.

Fassett repeatedly refers to us as a secular partisan lobby group. This is untrue. We are a Christian organization. Our founding document opens with the words, "Jesus Christ is Lord." All of our staff and board members are practicing church members. With rare exception on issues relating to overseas religious persecution, we do not endorse legislation. Our "lobbying" is almost entirely within churches.

So what is our message?

Of course we believe that the Gospel of Jesus Christ must instruct the political order and influence contemporary issues.

Our perspective on how the church best fulfills its political vocation is outlined in our founding statement: Within our several churches, disagreement about the meaning of social justice should not merely be tolerated; it should be cherished.

We are pledged to the goal that our churches be open churches. An open church engages sympathetically the diversity of Christian views both within and outside denominational structures. An open church welcomes dissent on contingent judgments about the right-ordering of society; this strengthens the search for truth and helps correct error. An open church makes decisions in the light of day, not in the shadowed corners of bureaucratic power. An open church has leaders eager to engage in the fullest consultation with all its members. An open church addresses social issues, not so much to advance a particular position as to inform and empower people to make their own decisions responsibly. An open church understands that the church speaks most effectively when the people who are the church do the speaking, and leaders speak more believably when they speak with the informed consent of those whom they would lead.

Most church members instinctively understand that there are limits to the appropriate political involvement of churches. This is why they do not understand the justification for church lobby offices such as the United Methodist Board of Church and Society. They do not agree with the often extreme and one-sided advocacy efforts of such agencies.

Thom Fassett's disconnect—and his real problem—is with those church members, and not with the Institute on Religion and Democracy.

Counter Response

THOM WHITE WOLF FASSETT

In their remarkable response to my brief narrative, officials of the Institute on Religion and Democracy (IRD) tell us more about themselves by their omissions than by their critique.

While claiming to be a Christian organization, IRD's advocacy is not transparently Christian, and their behavior lacks the qualities of fairness and honesty. Although not posing as a sect or a denomination as we commonly understand them, IRD, as a self-proclaimed religious organization, does not abide by creedal statements, confessions of faith, historic doctrinal statements or other distinguishing marks of Christian profession.

Like most mainline Christians, United Methodists understand that their church is the product of centuries of rich history and is centered in its historic doctrines, creeds and confessions. As one of the important historic streams of Christianity, Methodism finds it unique expression in the founding parents' passion for personal and social holiness. While all entities of The United Methodist Church (UMC) are guided by these theological principles, the General Board of Church and Society (GBCS) serves as a conscience of faith whose mandates are tied to the Social Principles of the UMC as well.

The small group of self-appointed overseers of the IRD, with few exceptions, has not changed in many years, and yet they claim to know the mind of the church. In sharp contrast, the more than 60 GBCS board members are democratically elected every four years. They are elected through an extensive process of democratic elections by annual, general and jurisdictional conferences. Contrary to IRD's assertion, the agency does not belong to Thom Fassett but to the United Methodist Church. By contrast, the IRD has no such democratic process of representation.

As a Christian organization, the UMC scrupulously monitors its inclusion of racial and ethnic minority people in the life of all of its structures. The IRD has no identifiable people of color in its organization, a fact that often is reflected in its opposition to UMC stands that strongly advocate for such persons and their communities. Racial overtones are sometimes not so subtle as when IRD issued press statements calling me "chief" of GBCS while correctly identifying, by title, the general secretaries of other United Methodist agencies. Only by implication could IRD be said to be racially inclusive as we find a sprinkling of people of color in their affiliates such as Renew, Good News and the Confessing Movement.

As a Christian organization, the UMC is passionate about "making disciples of Jesus Christ." The IRD has expressed no interest in converting people to Christ. Christian organizations follow Christian principles; IRD does not. While other unofficial UMC groups have worked with the GBCS, IRD refuses. When asked to work with GBCS against "most favored nation" status for China, we were told that even though IRD agreed with us, they would not work with us because their goal was to eliminate GBCS.

A Christian organization treats others as they would like to be treated. The IRD's demand for financial disclosure from UMC boards and agencies, which is open and freely available to any-one, has never been reciprocated by IRD. Their books are closed to public scrutiny. Saying they lobby only within the churches, its director was recently pictured in a pro-Israel demonstration on the steps of the U.S. Capitol. The IRD also lobbies members of Congress as a means of expressing their political views and seeks invitations to testify before congressional committees.

Praying with any president of the United States is a time of spiritual responsibility and mutual recognition of the power of God working through us. The IRD's claim that my prayer with the president was a partisan act demeans Christian practice and further defines their role as the "Harry and Louse" alarmists of the church spreading false tales. I have always gone anywhere, met with anyone, including Fidel Castro, to bring about the peaceful resolution of conflict and reduce the harm people and nations inflict upon one another because of their differences. I have been criticized for the company I keep. I recall that the Pharisees criticized Jesus for the company he kept. If the IRD represents the modern-day Pharisees, they would be well advised to hear Jesus' message in Luke 11:42-44, and so should we.

When Good News Is Bad News, or Working on a Coup D'etat

ANDREW WEAVER, NICOLE SEIBERT and FRED KANDELER

T he January/February 2004 issue of Zion's Herald published a special report on the activities of the Washington "think tank," the Institute on Religion and Democracy (IRD). The report, titled "Follow the Money," documented that The United Methodist Church (UMC), other mainline Protestant denominations, as well as the National Council of Churches of Christ have been the targets of an orchestrated attack by determined right-wing ideologues since 1981 (Weaver and Seibert, 2004a).

The IRD has relentlessly used unethical propaganda methods to carry out the radical political agenda of a handful of secular benefactors opposed to the churches' historic social witness (Weaver and Seibert, 2004b). This is particularly true of Mark Tooley, director of its UMAction arm, who worked for the CIA for eight years before being hired by IRD (UMAction, 2003).

In 1996, in a characteristically misleading fundraising letter, Tooley claimed that the UMC was supporting "Marxist guerrilla movements in Central America, violent revolution in southern Africa, halting U.S. defense programs, government-funded abortion, expanding the role of the federal government in the lives of ordinary Americans." He then asked, "Did membership in the United Methodist Church require loyalty to a political program of the far left?" Dr. John M. Swomley, Emeritus Professor of Social Ethics at St. Paul School of Theology in Kansas City, Missouri, observes that "Tooley, did not—and could not—document any of these assertions" (Swomley, 1996).

According to California-based investigative reporter Matt Smith, IRD and its allies' use of right-wing nonreligious foundation money to smear liberal church leaders through mailings, articles in IRD-aligned publications, press releases, and stories in secular newspapers and magazines has more in common with a CIA Third World destabilization campaign than ordinary civilized debate (Smith, 2004).

The IRD's patrons include the John M. Olin Foundation and ultra-conservative, Adolph Coors, Richard Mellon Scaife and Howard Ahmanson (Blumenthal, 2004; Cooperman, 2003; Howell, 1995; 2003; Media Transparency, 2004). Howard Ahmanson (whose wife, Roberta, serves on the IRD board of directors) has been a major financial backer of Christian Reconstructionism, a movement that works to replace American democracy with a fundamentalist theocracy (Robinson, 2002).

According to Christian Century, in the Reconstructionists' brave new America:

. . . minimum-wage laws and Social Security for younger workers would be eliminated; most old-age security would be covered by personal retirement plans or by care from adult children; and the federal government would play absolutely no part in regulating businesses, public education or welfare....all inheritance and gift taxes would be abolished, while income taxes would be no more than 10 percent of gross income (and then only until government was shrunk further). Gleaning for the poor on private farms after

harvesting would be encouraged (Shupe, 1989).

The article in Zion's Herald explained the interlocking relationships between the IRD and other self-styled "renewal"
groups in the UMC, like Good News and the Confessing
Movement, and how they amplify the distortions emanating
from IRD by regularly publishing its misrepresentations about
church leaders and programs (Weaver, and Seibert, 2004a; b).
IRD and its cohorts' underlying strategy is to delegitimize existing leadership in the eyes of church members, thereby fomenting a hostile takeover of mainline denominations (Institute on
Religion and Democracy, 2001; Goodstein and Kirkpatrick,
2004; Howell, 2003).

In August of 2004 two of the authors sent email copies of the
documented research on IRD and the right-wing attack on our
church to several thousand UMC leaders. Dozens of expressions
of appreciation for the work were received from all over the U.S.
There were also a few angry replies. By far the most hostile
response came from the then chair of the board of Good News,
Rev. Scott Field, senior minister at Wheatland Salem United
Methodist Church in Naperville, Illinois. He is also a designated
spokesperson for the Confessing Movement (Confessing
Movement Speakers Bureau, 2004).

The Rev. Scott Field wrote on Wednesday, August 25, 2004:

"…I am very well acquainted with IRD/UMAction (since I
am the chairperson of the Board of Directors of Good News)
and quite aware of the concerns raised by you and others
(*UM@Risk*, for example) about an alliance of knuckle-scraping
neo-literalists [terms Nicole Seibert and Andrew Weaver had
never seen or used] taking over the mainline Protestant denominations. Your 'loving concern' seems to me to be indicted by
your vicious attacks and unsubstantiated conspiracy theories.
(Brother Howell's book suffers from the same overreaching)…."

The "Brother Howell" to whom he refers to is the respected
journalist, long-time editor of Christianity and Crisis and

author of the well-researched and highly-documented *United Methodism@Risk: A Wake-Up Call*, written about the right-wing attack on the UMC (Howell, 2003).

We are not the only persons with whom Rev. Field has disagreed at whom he has lashed out. Before the 2004 UM General Conference in Pittsburgh, where he was "floor general" (as he was at the 2000 General Conference) for right-wing groups, including IRD, Good News and the Confessing Movement (Skinner, 2004), Rev. Field called those who disagreed with him "renegades and vigilantes making up their own rules" (Eckstrom, 2004).

Despite the overwhelming vote for unity at the end of the 2004 General Conference, 869 to 41, Rev. Field, the Good News board, and IRD continue to actively advocate and work for schism in the UMC. According to Christianity Today, during the conference's final session, "after almost 1,000 delegates stood, held hands, and sang, 'Blest be the Tie that Binds,' Rev. Fields, not an elected delegate, tried to down-play the call for unity and cooperation at General Conference" (Rutledge, 2004). He observed that the desire for unity "was understandable" saying, "When the institution is threatened, everyone dives to the middle." However, he added, "I think there is tremendous resonance [for separation talks] among folks in local churches." Christianity Today reported that at General Conference after the unity vote "both Field and Heidinger (president of Good News) agreed that institutional separation is all but inevitable" (Rutledge, 2004).

True to their word, Rev. Field and Good News, along with the IRD, whom they refer to as their "friends" (Good News Editorial Team, 2004), have continued to spearhead a call to implement options for schism that they judge has already occurred. This is revealed in a document entitled "Options for the Future" published by Good News shortly after the 2004 General Conference. In the pronouncement Rev. Field and colleagues lay out options for how to split if not outright shred the UMC (Dicken, Field,

Granger, and Lambrecht, 2004). These Good News leaders, including the present and two past chairs of the board, question whether continued "support of United Methodism is [any longer] a faithful response to the call of Christ" either for them personally or the UMC members in the congregations where they are appointed to serve (Dicken, Field, Granger, and Lambrecht, 2004).

The right-wing "options for the future" of the UMC include: 1) a continuation of current "renewal" attack strategies to form a dominant party in the church that can force the departure of those with whom they disagree through General Conference legislation and/or "loyalty oaths" that would supersede UM membership and ordination vows; 2) work for a bifurcated church by dismantling the historic structures in the denomination, thereby separating "Good News" followers from other baptized Christians with whom they disagree, while continuing to be United Methodism in name only; 3) the immediate restructuring of United Methodism as a "high-expectation covenant community," which has the same result as option 1, requiring those who do not conform to the "renewed covenant" to leave; and 4) structural divisions of United Methodism through either "amicable separation" or "voluntary departure" (Dicken, Field, Granger, and Lambrecht, 2004).

In "amicable separation," the UMC ceases to exist and individuals and congregations get to choose a new denomination of preference, clearing room for the division of properties, pensions and finances. The second scenario, "voluntary departure," offers the option for a church group to leave, most likely without property, pensions or finances ("voluntary departure" is the IRD preference for the folks with whom they disagree) (Tooley, 2004). Any one of these options would destroy the UMC.

They suggest several "tactics" to gain power to promote these goals, including redirection of funds and the threat of withdrawal of fellowship. They counsel that "redirection of funds" by local congregations is "essentially a pressure tactic, designed to pressure the denomination into taking steps that the congregation demands." They go on to say, "In order to be effective, there needs to be a substantial number of congregations taking this step in unison" (Dicken, Field, Granger, and Lambrecht, 2004).

They also advise, "Withdrawal of fellowship is another, similar tactic, whereby the congregation states it is out of fellowship (or communion) with a certain portion of the denomination. Like the redirection of funds, this is a pressure tactic designed as a means to another end. Most commonly, it is a prelude to separation" (Dicken, Field, Granger, and Lambrecht, 2004).

Rev. Field and his cohorts argue that networking with groups like Good News and the Confessing Movement "is a necessary prelude to most of the options…." However, it is acutely ironic that Good News—incorporated in 1967 as "A Forum for Scriptural Christianity"—would draw up and promote a 5,000-word plan for sedition using hardball power tactics in the Body of Christ without one word of biblical justification (Dicken, Field, Granger, and Lambrecht, 2004).

For a number of years, Rev. Field has been practicing what he preaches when it comes to defunding The United Methodist Church. Under Rev. Field's leadership between 1998 and 2003, his church in suburban Chicago paid only an average of 56 percent of its apportionments—and in 2003 that figure was a mere 31percent (Northern Illinois Conference, 1998-2003). It was in arrears in its apportionments nearly a quarter of a million dollars—($247,786) in the 6 years. During the same time, Rev. Field's compensation was paid in full to the tune of $431,477. Moreover in the same 6 years, Rev. Field's church paid $605,634 to causes outside the United Methodist connection. (Northern Illinois Conference, 1998-2003). These included missionaries sponsored by Ambassadors for Christ International headquartered in Tucker, Georgia (a group that teaches biblical "inerrancy in the original writings") and the Good News-endorsed non-UMC organization, Mission Society for United Methodists, based in Norcross, Georgia (Wheatland Salem United Methodist

Church, 2004).

Rev. Philip Granger, the president and CEO of the unauthorized Mission Society, as well as the chair of the Good News
board immediately prior to Rev. Field, is a co-author of the proposal to dismantle the UMC. A third author of "Options for the
Future," Rev. Tom Lambrecht, pastor of Faith Community
United Methodist Church in Greenville, Wisconsin, was vice-
chair of the Good News board until he assumed full board leadership in January 2005 (Dicken, Field, Granger, and Lambrecht,
2004). The fourth and lead author of the declaration is Rev.
Mark Dicken of Clarksvillie, Indiana, who practiced law prior to
entering ordained ministry (Dicken, 1998).

Strategies proposed by Good News and IRD to dismantle the
UMC have been in the works for years prior to the current
"options" scheme. One proposal would defund the UMC seminaries (Institute on Religion and Democracy, 2004). Good News
and IRD advocated for a seminary "voucher" system at the 2004
General Conference that would drain money from the UMC
seminaries (Field, 2004). According to the Association of United
Methodist Theological Seminaries representing all 13 UMC theological schools, the "voucher" scheme would significantly dam-
age 12 UMC schools of theology and out-right destroy its only
predominantly African-American seminary, Gammon
Theological Seminary in Atlanta (Henderson, 2003).

It is noteworthy that Mark Tooley, a long-time board member
of Good News, while speaking for IRD, said in June of 2001 that
UMC seminaries need to be "reigned in" (People for the
American Way, 2001). He went on to say that if "radical" UMC
seminaries do not conform to IRD expectations, "church
reformers" should work harder toward "cutting them loose from
any affiliation with our church." The "voucher plan" that Good
News and IRD are striving to implement would be a mechanism
to do just that. What is more, if all the UM clergy follow Rev.
Field's example as church leaders and pay only 56 percent of
their apportionments, it could rapidly close down all UMC

Seminaries and Africa University.

The renowned Wesley scholar, Albert C. Outler, told memorable stories in class. One of his favorites was about a letter the president of Southern Methodist University, Willis Tate, had received from a United Methodist mother in a small east Texas town. Her son was enrolled for the fall term, and she wrote that she was concerned that he have a college roommate who could set a good example for him. She did not want her son to be exposed to bad influences, such as rough language or the distraction of girls who might lead him astray. At the end was a postscript: "The reason I am writing you is that this is the first time my boy has been away from home, except for the three years he spent in the U.S. Marines."

Those of us who are concerned for the welfare of the UMC, which has nurtured generations of Americans in the Christian faith, need to stop being as naïve as the mother in Dr. Outler's story. We must be alert and steadfast when people are willing to advocate and use hardball political tactics to dismantle our historic, mainline denomination and connection of churches across the world. These people are deadly serious and determined. The Bible is clear that we must protect the sheep from wolves that would devour them, and Christ warns us about false prophets.

"15 Watch out for false prophets. They come to you in sheep clothing, but inwardly they are ferocious wolves. 16 By their fruit you will recognize them. Do people pick grapes from thornbushes, or figs from thistles?" — *Matthew 7:15-16 (NIV)*

We need to pray without ceasing for our brothers and sisters in Christ who believe that one must destroy the UMC church to save it. Warlike tactics and calls for schism are to be rebuked, as Philip Otterbein and John Wesley did in their time.

Bishop Kenneth L. Carder, Professor of the Practice of Pastoral Formation at Duke Divinity School, recently wrote this:

"In (his sermon) 'On Schism' Wesley warns that hostile contention within the church is contrary to God's commands, violates the meaning of Christian love, and creates a stumbling block for the world. He warns: 'O beware, I will not say of forming, but of countenancing or abetting any parties in a Christian society!' Echoing Jesus, Wesley writes, 'Happy is he who attains the character of peacemaker in the church of God.' " (Carter, 2005).

We must have the clear-eyed resolve to resist these tactics for the sake of those who will come after us. The next generation of souls will need the Christian witness and power of the Holy Spirit that is found in The United Methodist Church and other mainline denominations, and they need our faithfulness now.

References

Blumenthal, M. (2004). "Avenging angel of the religious right." Retrieved on January 6, 2004, http://archive.salon.com/news/feature/2004/01/06/ahmanson/index.html.

Carter, K.L. (2005). Personal communication. Martin Luther King Day, March 17, 2005.

Confessing Movement Speakers Bureau. (2004). Retrieved on December 30, 2004, http://www.confessingumc.org/speakers.html.

Dicken, M. (1998). A Pastoral Response to the Jury s Verdict Delivered at Edwardsville United Methodist Church, Georgetown, Indiana, Sunday, March 15, 1998. Retrieved on December 30, 2004, http://www.confessingumc.org/sermon_dicken.html.

Dicken, M., Field, S., Granger, P., and Lambrecht, T. (2004). "Options for the Future, With Some Strategic Implications," Summer 2004. Retrieved on December 30, 2004, http://www.nicvoice.org/GC2004%20Updates56.htm.

Eckstrom, K. (2004). "Protestants: Gay issues will dominate Methodists agenda." Religion News Service, April 24, 2004. Retrieved on December 29, 2004, http://www.dfw.com/mld/pioneerpress/living/religion/8504324.htm?1c.

Field, S. (2004). Good News at General Conference faithful disciples - a renewed church (Jan/Feb). Retrieved on December 31, 2004, http://www.goodnewsmag.org/magazine/1JanFeb/jf04position.htm.

Good News Editorial Team. (2004). The UM Decision 2004 team effort. Retrieved on December 30, 2004, http://www.goodnewsmag.org/magazine/3MayJune/mj04team_effort.htm.

Goodstein, L. and Kirkpatrick, D.D. (2004). "Conservative Group Amplifies Voice of Protestant Orthodoxy," New York Times, May 22, 2004, page 1.

Henderson, B. (2003). The United Methodist ministerial education fund. From the Perkins School of Theology Alumni Association. Retrieved on December 2, 2003, from http://www.NWHillsUMC.org.

Howell, L. (2003). *United Methodism @ Risk: A wake up call.* Kingston, NY: Information Project for United Methodists.

Howell, L. (1995). "Funding the war of ideas: A report to the United Church Board for Homeland Ministries." Cleveland, OH: United Church Board for Homeland Ministries.

Institute on Religion and Democracy. (2001). http://www.4religious-right.info/internal_ document_ird.html, Institute on Religion and Democracy s reforming America s churches project: 2001-2004, executive summary. Retrieved on September 30, 2003, http://www.theocracy-watch.org/internal_document_ird.html.

Institute on Religion and Democracy. (2004). A Reform Agenda for United Methodists. Retrieved on December 31, 2004, http://www.ird-renew.org/About/AboutList.cfm?c=27.

Media Transparency. (2004). The Money behind the media. Institute on Religion and Democracy, Inc. Retrieved on December 31, 2004, http://www.mediatransparency.org/about.htm" http://www.mediatransparency.org/about.htm.

Northern Illinois Conference of the United Methodist Church (1998-2003). Chicago, IL.: Journal.

People for the American Way. (2001). Colorado-Hostile Climate, Denver: Institute on Religion and Democracy attacks liberal seminary, Retrieved on December 30, 2004, http://www.pfaw.org/pfaw/general/default.aspx?oid=3601#.

Robinson, B.A. (2002). Christian reconstructionism, dominion theology, and theonomy. Ontario Consultants on Religious Tolerance. Retrieved on November 14, 2003, from www.religioustolerance.org.

Rutledge, K.K. (2004). Pondering a Divorce: Some United Methodists think their differences are irreconcilable, Christianity Today, July, 48(7), 50.

Shupe, A. (1989). The Reconstructionist Movement on the New Christian Right. Christian Century, October 4, 1989, pp. 880-882.

Skinner, C. (2004). Methodists face possible church split over gay rights. Illinois Leader.com, May 06, 2004. Retrieved on December 29, 2004, http://www.illinoisleader.com/news/newsview.asp?c=14628.

Smith, M. (2004). Institute of Hate, San Francisco Weekly, February

25, 2004.

Swomley, J. M. (1996). Covert ops, Christian-style - former CIA operative Mark Tooley now works for the religious right.
http://www.findarticles.com/p/articles/mi_m1374 Humanist, Retrieved on December 30, 2004,
http://www.findarticles.com/p/articles/mi_m1374/is_n4_v56/ai_18501023.

Tooley, M. (2004). IRD Urges Gracious Exit from United Methodism for Pro- Gay Advocates. Retrieved on December 30, 2004,
http://www.ird-renew.org/News/News.cfm?ID=970&c=3.

UMAction. (2003). Links to the writings of Mark Tooley. United Methodists Affirming Christ s Teachings in our Nation. Retrieved on October 8, 2003, from http://umaction.org/index.htm.

Weaver, A.J., and Seibert, N. (2004a) Follow the Money: The well heeled attack on The United Methodist Church Zion s Herald.(Jan/Feb, 2004). This can be found online at http://www.zion-sherald.org/Jan2004_specialreport.html.

Weaver, A.J. and Seibert, N. (2004b) Church and Scaife, Secular conservative philanthropies waging unethical campaign to take over United Methodist Church. Mediatransparency.org, August 2, 2004. Retrieved on December 30, 2004,
http://www.mediatransparency.org/stories/irdi.html.

Wheatland Salem United Methodist Church. (2004).Naperville, IL. Check out Wheatland Salem Church [Faith Promise]. Retrieved on December 30, 2004,
http://www.wheatlandsalem.org/missions/faith_promise.htm.

A Good News Response
to Recent Accusations
Adopted by the Executive Committee
of the Good News Board, March 8, 2005

Recent articles and unsolicited emails being disseminated via the Internet have attacked the credibility, purpose, and strategy of Good News, in its attempt to bring reform and renewal within The United Methodist Church. These attacks have reached the level of a secular political smear campaign (including accusations that evangelical renewal groups are "wolves in sheep's clothing" and "false prophets"). Since the misinformation and innuendos contained in these articles and emails could confuse or dishearten evangelicals concerned about the renewal of the Church as well as distract others from the pressing issues of unity and diversity within The United Methodist Church, Good News must respond to the claims made about us.

Claim:
The Institute on Religion and Democracy (IRD) acts as a coordinating influence on the various United Methodist evan-

gelical renewal groups, using them to publish false information and providing funding and direction to these groups.

Fact:

Good News and the other evangelical renewal groups are independent organizations, each with its own purposes and emphases within the overall cause of renewal within The United Methodist Church. Like the self-identified "progressive" caucuses and publications within United Methodism, evangelical renewal groups do seek to accomplish common goals, but each group has its own board of directors, its own policies, and its own positions on the issues. There are times when the groups disagree with one another on policy or strategy. No one group provides overall direction or coordination for the others. Good News receives no funding from IRD or other evangelical renewal groups. Several groups did reimburse Good News for their share of expenses in our joint efforts at General Conference.

It is worth mentioning that Good News has been in ministry since 1967, predating the IRD by 14 years and the Confessing Movement by 27 years. We have in the past and continue to encourage thousands of United Methodists to remain within our denomination, working faithfully in their local churches and seeking renewal at every level. We have operated in the light of day from the beginning, making our views and concerns known, publishing them in our magazine, and advocating them at General Conferences as early as 1972.

Claim:

Good News receives significant funding from ultra-right-wing foundations with a political agenda. Good News is linked with Christian Reconstructionism, "a movement that works to replace American democracy with a fundamentalist theocracy."

Fact:

The vast majority of Good News' income comes from individuals and churches within the UMC who believe in the cause of renewal. We do receive some gifts from individuals who channel their giving through their own personal or small private foundations. Up to now, Good News has not received grants from any major secular or political foundations, nor from any groups or individuals unrelated to The United Methodist Church. Our audited financial statements are available to the public. We are not part of any conservative or right-wing political agenda to take over the United States or The United Methodist Church. It is bizarre, even laughable, to say that Good News' renewal work is part of a conspiracy to usher in a fundamentalist theocracy in the United States. We simply long to see The United Methodist Church totally committed to Jesus Christ and his mission of love and salvation for the world, as outlined for us in the Scriptures.

Claim:
Good News actively advocates and works for schism in the UMC.

Fact:
Good News has never advocated schism or separation in the UMC, nor do we advocate it under current conditions. We are distressed that certain leaders and segments of the church are proclaiming a theology that contradicts our established standards of doctrine. Indeed, John Wesley identified the true "separatists" as "those, and those only, …who either renounce [the church's] fundamental doctrines, or refuse to join in her public worship" (Letter to Rev. Samuel Walker, September 24, 1755). Furthermore, we are deeply concerned that some self-identified "progressive" portions of the church are advocating disobedience to the clear and longstanding provisions in the Book of Discipline regarding human sexuality. We wonder how those who are working to change or violate the basic covenant of United Methodism can continue to live with integrity long-term within The United Methodist Church.

In fact, the idea of "amicable separation" arose for discussion at the 2004 General Conference only after several "progressive" leaders stated bluntly in conversation that it really did not matter what General Conference said or did on the matter of homo-sexuality, they would not abide by it. This raises the question of how to have a covenant connection when a group within the connection says it will not abide by the covenant. Indeed, from time to time, in response to what we have understood to be egregious breaches of the covenant of the clergy, we have echoed the scriptural question, "How can two walk together unless they be agreed?" (Amos 3:3) and Jesus' observation that a house divided against itself will not stand (Matthew 12:25).

However, Good News does not believe that current conditions warrant separation, unless the "progressive" wing of our church concludes it can no longer abide by the Book of Discipline. Good News continues to believe that the only viable basis for unity within The United Methodist Church is commitment to believing and proclaiming the doctrine of our church, as defined by our doctrinal standards, and to living the faith in "Scriptural holiness," not in capitulating to the thoughts and spirit of our time.

The paper, "Options for the Future," which is selectively quoted in some of the articles and emails, was written following the 2004 General Conference to help the Good News board examine its options in continuing to work for the renewal of The United Methodist Church. The paper was significantly influenced by Lyle Schaller's landmark book, *The Ice Cube Is Melting*. (It is highly inconsistent for critics of Good News to fail to address Schaller's book, which forms the background for much of the paper.) The paper was a study document not meant for public distribution, and it did not reflect the position of the Good News board. Based on the study of that document, the board at its August 2004 meeting declared, "In recognition of the threats to the unity of The United Methodist Church today, Good News will begin to examine and explore the issues raised by the proposal for amicable separation and the resolution on unity during the 2004 General Conference. This exploration will be a major emphasis of Good News' renewal work during this current quadrennium." Since that time, the Good News board has embarked on a study process that will help to inform our future strategic decisions regarding the work of renewal. No decisions have been made, nor have any options been chosen at this time. None of the options regarding structural change in the UMC considered in Options for the Future are currently being advocated by Good News.

Claim:
Good News' leaders are unsupportive of the denomination and support "causes outside the United Methodist connection," including "unauthorized" groups, such as the Mission Society for United Methodists.

Fact:
As stated above, many board members of Good News over the years have been respected leaders within their annual conference and the general church. Some have been district superintendents or chairs of conference agencies, others have served as directors of general agencies, and at least one has become the general secretary of a general agency. Many have been elected as delegates to General and Jurisdictional Conference. Board members are often active participants in evangelism and mission programs sponsored by The United Methodist Church.

It has been common in our history for United Methodist churches to support mission causes beyond the United Methodist connection. Groups like the Red Cross, Wycliffe Bible Translators, the Gideons, Habitat for Humanity, and many others have received support. There is no requirement that non-United Methodist groups receive some sort of "approval" in order to be fit recipients of UM mission giving. Many general agencies of the church, including the Board of Church and Society and the Board of Global Ministries, contribute to groups and ministries with no connection to the UMC. And regarding "unauthorized" groups, the Methodist Federation for Social Action is just as much an "unauthorized" group as the Mission Society for United Methodists.

The Mission Society was formed 21 years ago by pastors and laity to provide an opportunity for churches and individuals with a heart for evangelism, church planting and leadership development as well as ministries of compassion, to become involved in global missions. The Mission Society views itself as a supplemental mission organization and NOT as a replacement for the General Board of Global Ministries. In the 21 years since its founding, the Mission Society has deployed over 325 missionaries, with 180+ currently serving on the field. In addition, the Mission Society works with over 3,200 indigenous ministry partners in the 31 countries where it has personnel stationed. It accomplishes this with only 20 support personnel in the Norcross, Georgia, office. The Mission Society is a charter member of the Evangelical Council for Financial Accountability (ECFA), and its audited financial statements are available to the public.

Claim:

Good News engages in "hardball political tactics to dismantle our historic, mainline denomination." Good News seeks to "delegitimize existing leadership [of the UMC] in the eyes of church members, thereby fomenting a hostile takeover of mainline denominations."

Fact:

For over 50 years, the self-identified "progressive" elements of The United Methodist Church and its predecessors have worked behind the scenes to organize and control the agenda and actions of the church. They are now dismayed to see evangelicals successfully organizing to promote the agenda of renewal, reform, and faithfulness to Scripture. Good News seeks to advocate for reform and renewal and to organize the grassroots of the church to achieve that end. This is no different from the political activity of any other group in the church, including the past and present actions of the "progressive" United Methodists. Although we have not always succeeded, we try to exercise our political and legislative activity within the church with a

74

Christlike spirit of love and humility.

The United Methodist Church is a political organization, as well as a church, the Body of Christ. Whenever large numbers of people try to work together in an organization, political activity (organizing, lobbying representatives, writing letters and legislation, working to elect like-minded persons, etc.) is normally part of the process. What we seek to do is have a legislative and political process within the church that operates on Christian principles and Christlike attitudes. We regret that for many years, evangelicals were not involved in this dimension of the church's life. Thankfully, that is no longer the case. We apologize for those times when we have failed to live up to those Christlike standards, and we prayerfully seek to "go on to perfection."

* * *

It is our opinion that the issues of unity and diversity among United Methodists have reached a point for critical and thoroughgoing reflection. We have committed ourselves to study, prayer, and Christian conferencing in order to discern the times and seek faithful responses to the opportunities before us all. We invite laity and clergy across the denomination to consider our church's course, tone down the rhetoric, and cease the attacks. We welcome genuine dialog in appropriate forums for a wide-ranging conversation on the issues of what holds us together and what pulls us apart.

"Crashing" the Farewell Party

LINDA S. RHODES

In the midst of nearly 400 people at a retirement banquet celebrating the ministry of Bishop C. Joseph Sprague, a young man dressed in a white shirt and black suit began to attract attention. He photographed and tape recorded every speaker. He noted who was in attendance. He took in the whole event in silence—until Bishop Sprague blew his cover and recognized him as John Lomperis, a member of the staff of the Institute on Religion and Democracy (IRD).

The IRD, based in Washington, D.C., is a right-wing organization created to target progressive policies, people and structures within United Methodist, Presbyterian and Episcopal churches. The IRD website says it is working to "reform the social and political witness" of these churches. Specifically, it objects to Protestant churches' involvement in what it calls "leftist crusades" such as "feminism, environmentalism, pacifism, multi-culturalism, revolutionary socialism, sexual liberation and so forth."

The IRD says it works through "conservative renewal groups"

within each denomination to try to effect the changes it desires.

Lomperis works for Mark Tooley, director of UMAction, the department of the IRD that focuses on: United Methodists. For the last eight years, Tooley and his staff have criticized, defamed and hounded Bishop Sprague through articles in their UMAction newsletter and on the IRD website. So it shocked many of us attending Bishop Sprague's retirement dinner when this blatant enemy of everything Bishop Sprague has stood for throughout his ministry "crashed" this final farewell for the bishop's friends and family.

When I asked Lomperis why he was there, he immediately began defending his right to attend the dinner. He said, "This is a public event, open to all United Methodists." Well, that explained why he was allowed in the door. Actually, as far as I know, the event organizers welcomed anyone who wished to purchase a ticket. But that didn't answer my question: Why was he there? The rest of us were there to honor Bishop Sprague, to thank him for his ministry and witness among us, to celebrate his life and work. Was that why Lomperis had come? To honor the bishop? I doubted it.

But Lomperis kept insisting, "I have a right to be here because I'm a United Methodist."

I asked him which United Methodist congregation he belongs to. Uh, well ... It turns out he is not a member of any United Methodist congregation. He said he attends an "evangelical, ecumenical church." But he still claims to be a United Methodist. When I tried to give him the benefit of the doubt, suggesting that perhaps he is a United Methodist "in name only" because he doesn't attend a United Methodist church, he had the audacity to declare that, yes, he is "just like the other 8.5 million United Methodists in the country."

Oh, really? I think the young Mr. Lomperis is "unclear on the concept" of what it means to be a United Methodist.

Lomperis seems unaware that those of us who really are United Methodists praise God and lift our prayers in worship in

United Methodist churches, serve as liturgists, prepare worship centers, sing in choirs, teach Sunday school classes for children and adults, maintain church buildings, and lead youth groups.

Lomperis seems unaware that those of us who really are United Methodists read and study Scripture through Disciple Bible Study classes, Schools of Christian Mission, Walks to Emmaus, Alpha, and programs of United Methodist Men and United Methodist Women.

Lomperis seems unaware that those of us who really are United Methodists participate in Volunteer-In-Mission work trips, traveling around the country and around the world to help build houses, repair homes damaged by floods and tornadoes, feed the hungry, work in hospitals and clinics, assist emerging new congregations and testify to the great love of Jesus Christ.

Lomperis seems unaware that those of us who really are United Methodists donate the money that supports more than 1,000 missionaries serving in 70 countries. And that—inside the U.S. alone—we help fund 65 community centers, 65 hospitals and health-care facilities, 225 retirement and long-term-care facilities, more than 100 colleges and universities, and 13 theological schools.

And it's obvious that Lomperis was unaware that those of us who really are United Methodists have "open hearts, open minds and open doors."

But Lomperis saw United Methodism in action, because despite the fact that he is not a United Methodist, despite the fact that he was not there to honor Bishop Sprague and had come to the dinner under false pretenses, despite the fact that he is part of an organization that has harassed Bishop Sprague for the past eight years, despite the fact that he seems to know nothing about the denomination he is trying to destroy—John Lomperis was not only allowed into Bishop Sprague's retirement dinner, but also was greeted cordially and treated with respect—at least by everyone but me!

The bishop shook his hand and said that even though he

worked for an organization about which Bishop Sprague could say nothing good, Lomperis himself was welcome. Bishop Sprague treated Lomperis as a child of God—greeting him with graciousness and warmth.

The Rev. Deborah Fisher, senior pastor of First United Methodist Church in Downers Grove and co-chair of the dinner, asked Lomperis if he had heard anything that night that changed his mind about Bishop Sprague. Lomperis admitted he was surprised that he had not heard "any evangelical bashing." Fisher told Lomperis that in all her years of working with Bishop Sprague, she had never heard any "evangelical bashing" either behind closed doors or in public.

Of course, the only things Lomperis heard at the banquet, the only things said by anyone there, were praise and thanks for the mission and ministry of a humble servant of God.

Dr. Phil Blackwell, senior pastor of First United Methodist Church of Chicago (The Chicago Temple) and co-chair of the dinner, suggested that maybe the retirement banquet could be, for Lomperis, a Damascus Road experience like that of Saul, the persecutor of Christians who became Paul, the great missionary who spread Christianity to the gentiles. Saul saw the light of Christ, turned his life around and quit persecuting Christians. Maybe Lomperis can do the same.

I pray that it will be so.

Reprinted by permission from the August 13, 2004, issue of The Reporter of the Northern Illinois Conference of The United Methodist Church.

The Ominous Cost of Renewal

ANDREW J. WEAVER

In the January/February 2004 issue of Zion's Herald my colleague, Nicole Seibert, and I published a special report on the activities of the Institute on Religion and Democracy (IRD). We documented how the IRD is primarily funded by right-wing secular foundations with an ultra-conservative political agenda. We also showed how IRD is being used as a hammer against The United Methodist Church (UMC) by two other conservative, self-styled "renewal" groups, Good News and the Confessing Movement. We have been contacted by dozens of concerned UMC leaders who have expressed appreciation for this information, several of whom say they will help us to continue our ongoing investigations.

In the article we noted that Thomas C. Oden, as the chair of IRD and a member of the board of directors of the Confessing Movement, is the leading advocate for the use of the "nuclear option" by the renewal groups in their culture wars with fellow United Methodists. This is described in a document titled "The

Trust Clause Governing Use of Property in The United Methodist Church" that can be found on both the Good News and Confessing Movement Web sites. Dr. Oden argues that "True Methodists" need to challenge the church's trust clause to claim United Methodist assets. He argues that he and his colleagues in the renewal groups have the church's only correct theological formulations and therefore should lay claim to the church's property though the courts.

Guess what? According to Good News, some United Methodists have taken Dr. Oden's strategy seriously. Good News has announced on its Web site that a "first strike" has taken place in Kansas and Alaska. A 125-member congregation in Gove, Kansas, for example, has voted to disassociate from the denomination for allegedly violating doctrinal standards by "allowing and condoning the following: same-sex unions, homosexual ordination, Sophia worship, goddess worship, Wicca worship, pagan practices, anti-trinitarianism, [and] opposition to the virgin birth and the deity of Christ." A hearing date on the lawsuit filed against the denomination has not been set.

What does this mean? For starters, if this litigious strategy is repeated by other disgruntled groups across the denomination, it will drain millions of dollars in legal fees from the church's invaluable ministries and tarnish its public witness.

But a deeper implication of such aggressive, even hostile, behavior by Christians toward fellow Christians is posed by the following: What sort of church will we have if bitter, angry and vengeful people succeed in taking over its institutions and assets?

If Dr. Oden and his allies in the renewal camp are permitted to dismember the church in this manner, it will be nothing less than a crime against our heritage. For perhaps the first time in history, "renew" will be synonymous with "destroy."

Why the Right Proposed Schism

SCOTT CAMPBELL

As United Methodists we remain in covenant with one another, even in the midst of disagreement, and affirm our commitment to work together for our common mission of making disciples throughout the world.

– The United Methodist Church 2004 General Conference

John Dart, writing in the June 1, 2004 issue of The Christian Century, commented on the seemingly incongruous behavior of certain conservative leaders in The United Methodist Church when they floated a resolution to split the denomination on the same day they had won major victories around the issue of homosexuality at the recently concluded General Conference of the church. "The idea was startling because conservatives were flushed with success, and odds favor their making gains in the future," he wrote.

The idea is only startling if one supposes that homosexuality is the foundational concern of these leaders. It is not.

Homosexuality has been the foot in the door that certain leaders on the right hoped would open the way for much more substantive church reform. Many of them believed that conservative victories in Cleveland in 2000 would be the precursor to such change in Pittsburgh in 2004. Those hopes were dashed.

Homosexuality has indeed proved to be an effective rallying cry for the leaders of the renewal movement, but victories in this area have not translated into meaningful change in other parts of the church. The legislative agenda of Good News, a prominent conservative renewal group in the church, was resoundingly rejected by the General Conference. The group submitted legislation under ten headings, ranging from what they called "Doctrinal Integrity" to "Christian Witness in the Muslim World." Nearly all of their proposals were defeated, most of them not making it out of various legislative committees.

Major initiatives around enforcing doctrinal fidelity, reshaping judicial processes, changing the accountability of the Women's Division, refocusing the Board of Church and Society, redistributing scholarship funds, changing the definition of "self-avowed practicing homosexuals," eliminating mandatory support of the general church budget, reconstituting the University Senate, and prohibiting United Methodist membership in the Religious Coalition for Reproductive Choice were all soundly rejected.

Conservative renewal leaders now find themselves in a most uncomfortable place. They have a denomination that rejects the ordination of homosexuals, but which has enacted almost nothing else on their reform agenda and doesn't seem inclined to do so any time in the near future. The church remains solidly centrist by almost every measure. What is more, it continues to lean to the left in terms of most of its social policy positions.

It is in this context that one must understand the proposal that was floated to divide the church. The late Rev. William Hinson introduced the idea by expressing his concern for persons who had been wounded by the church's position on homosexuality. "Who are we to step on their dreams?" he wondered, neglecting to mention that conservatives had spoken passionately on the floor two days earlier against recognizing that faithful Christians disagree on this issue. His initiative, however, had little to do with homosexuality. It was a calculated political move to gain influence in an ongoing struggle to shape the future of The United Methodist Church. As it turns out, it was a move that may have backfired.

By offering "amicable separation" to persons discouraged and defeated by the votes on homosexuality, certain conservative leaders hoped that a significant minority of the church, i.e. the progressives, would decide they had had enough and would be ready to leave. One strategy of these leaders appears to be to make life in the church so intolerable for gay and lesbian persons and their supporters that the price of staying will eventually become too high. They have chosen to use homosexuality because it is an issue around which they have a voting majority, largely due to an affinity that they share on this issue with overseas delegates, who now comprise nearly one-fifth of the voting members of the General Conference. With this majority they have attempted to keep ratcheting up the pressure.

Diane Knippers, president of the Institute on Religion and Democracy (IRD), a conservative reform group that is advocating for schism in The United Methodist Church, the Presbyterian Church USA and the Episcopal Church, made a revealing comment in a May 22, 2004, New York Times article. "Rather than be embroiled in legal battles in church courts over sexuality, let's find a gracious way to say, 'we will let you (liberals) leave this system because you believe it violates your conscience.'"

The same article quotes Alfred F. Ross, president of the Institute for Democracy Studies, a liberal New York think tank, who understands the IRD's agenda to be a part of a larger political strategy of the secular right wing. "The mainline denominations are a strategic piece on the chess board that the right wing is trying to dominate. It will give them access to three important pieces. One is the Sunday pulpit. Two is millions of dollars of capacity internally, with control of church newsletters and pension funds. And three is foreign missions."

For some United Methodist conservative renewal leaders the picture is not a happy one. For more than 30 years they have been trying to reshape the priorities of the denomination with little to show for their efforts. It is out of their frustration at such limited gains that the resolution to divide the church should be understood. One can only imagine how discouraging it was to have their proposal for schism utterly repudiated by more than 95 percent of the delegates, who declared that, in spite of real disagreements, they would continue as one church.

The board of Good News has tried to put a positive spin on this outcome, even though two of its leaders, the Rev. James Heidinger and the Rev. Scott Field, were among those who proposed the split in the first place. The board's affirmation of the covenant resolution, however, rings hollow. After declaring that they affirm the statement that was passed by the General Conference, they go on to add conditions: "We will uphold the unity of The United Methodist Church as long as our common covenant is upheld by the actions of the church. Where entities of the church take actions that contravene our covenant and Discipline, however, we will recognize the splintering of that unity."

Their full statement is replete with the language of fear about potential violations of the covenant. It talks a good deal about enforcement and upholding law. This is a group that appears not very secure in its ability to persuade others of the power of its vision right now.

Given the failure of the conservative renewal groups to significantly influence the shape of the denomination, it is not surprising that some among them would resort to desperate measures to advance their agenda. It seems crucial that progressive and moderate United Methodists resist the temptation to accept short-sighted, quick fix solutions like "amicable separation" for dealing with differences in the church. The price of defecting would be enormous, virtually guaranteeing that United

Methodism would follow the Southern Baptists down the road towards theological extremism.

It is entirely understandable that those being most directly harmed by the church's position on homosexuality would seek relief from the struggle. And it would be impossible to fault those who choose to leave the denomination on grounds that spiritual violence is being done to them or to those they love. On the other hand, for those who are able to stay with the struggle, the benefits to the church and to society will be great. By refusing to cede control to persons who would narrow the vision of the church, moderate and progressive United Methodists will leave a church to their children and their children's children that will honor the fullness of our Wesleyan heritage.

Good News has been fond of quoting John Wesley concerning "the faith once delivered to the saints." We would do well to remember the whole context in which that phrase appears in Wesley's "Catholic Spirit" sermon:

And now run the race which is set before thee, in the royal way of universal love. Take heed, lest thou be either wavering in thy judgment, or straitened in thy bowels: but keep an even pace, rooted in the faith once delivered to the saints, and grounded in love, in true catholic love, till thou art swallowed up in love for ever and ever!

Interview: Diane Knippers

STEPHEN SWECKER

At the time of her untimely death on April 18, 2005, Diane Knippers was President of the Institute on Religion and Democracy in Washington, D.C. Before joining the IRD in 1982, she was Associate Executive Secretary of Good News and Editor of Good News magazine. Mrs. Knippers graduated in 1972 from Asbury College and from the University of Tennessee in 1974 with a M.A. in Sociology. She has written for such publications as The Wall Street Journal, The Weekly Standard and Crisis. Mrs. Knippers directed the Episcopal Action program of the IRD, which seeks to reform the public witness of the Episcopal Church, of which she was a member. Zion's Herald editor Stephen Swecker interviewed Mrs. Knippers at her Washington, D.C. office on Dec. 14, 2004.

ZH: Let's start off with the recent national election results. I'm assuming you're pleased.

DK: Well, personally I am pleased. It's probably not a shock to anyone that I'm a supporter of George Bush.

ZH: Among the characterizations of the IRD have been that it's the "White House Seminary" and "the Republican Party at prayer." What do you say to that?

DK: Well, I think that's not true. I was actually invited to the White House more under Carter's tenure than I have been under either of the Bush administrations. We really just want the church to have an impact on social and political issues.

ZH: How do you suppose that can happen when President Bush, whom you support, does not invite his own United Methodist Church leaders to the White House or engage publicly with social and political statements from his own church?

DK: Well, I think that's not true. I was actually invited to the White House more under Clinton's tenure than I have been under either Bush administration. IRD's focus isn't on the administration, but on the church having an impact on social and political issues.

ZH: Flipping from the present to the past for a moment, to the origins of the IRD in 1981: the public record tells the story of United Methodist layman David Jessup and his role in founding the IRD. But, Mr. Jessup, a relative unknown, soon was joined by prominent Catholics such as Michael Novak, George Weigel and Richard John Neuhaus [who later became a Catholic], to name a few. These were people with no connection at all to the denomination and who remain important in the IRD today. Can you explain why people with no ties to the UMC are so concerned with its affairs, its organization, criticizing its leaders and so on?

DK: Well, I think that our board members are concerned about the influence of the mainline Protestant churches in general, politically. I don't think they're any more concerned about The United Methodist Church than they are about the Episcopal Church or the Presbyterian Church.

ZH: But, that's the point, isn't it? These are mainline Protestant churches and those guys are Catholics who are going after them. Do you suppose the IRD could have gotten the funding that it got back in the early days from outside secular sources had you not had some big names like Novak and Weigel? What was their interest in mainline churches?

DK: Well, they're ecumenists. They're concerned about the integrity of the church, they're concerned that the church…I mean, at the time we were starting, our main concern was foreign policy, and the compelling interest of those members at the beginning was church support for Marxist-Leninist causes. These are Christian citizens who are concerned about the witness of the church, and that was the motivation.

ZH: One of the stated purposes of the IRD is holding mainline Protestant churches accountable to their members. Now, I have to press this. You have on your board of advisors prominent Catholics and people from the Jewish community. What is their interest as IRD members in directly going to Protestant mainline churches to hold them accountable—but not to their own faith communities? Where does the legitimacy for doing that come from? If the shoe were on the other foot, and you had an organization of self-appointed Protestants attacking Catholic or Jewish organizations, how do you think that would go down?

DK: Well, I think there are a couple of things you have to understand about the way we do it. I mean, the IRD is concerned about the reform of the churches' social and political witness. That's everyone's concern and witness. I mean, I tell my Southern Baptist friends they need to be concerned about the witness to the gospel of the Episcopal Church. I'm desperately concerned about the Roman Catholic Church. I think all Christians are embarrassed and angry over the sex scandals in the Catholic Church.

ZH: Do you push that concern as actively as you push, say, taking action against gay clergy in the Protestant churches?

DK: No, and that's because our major programmatic focus is clearly on the mainline Protestant churches. The point I'm trying to make is that it's not illegitimate, particularly in an age of ecumenism, that Christians should be concerned about the witness of other churches.

ZH: Do you think most of the people in the churches that IRD is addressing regarding accountability realize they are being advised by an agency whose directors are in no way representative of their church?

DK: It's perfectly clear on our Web site; we're very proud of our board. The analogy that I make is that people in the mainline are used to working ecumenically, they're used to being involved with the National Council of Churches and the World Council of Churches.

ZH: But the IRD is highly critical of precisely these groups. From the outside, it appears the IRD itself does not actually promote ecumenism except in a narrow sense that it includes Catholics and Jews on its board.

DK: No, no, no, no! I am an enthusiastic ecumenist. I'm angry because I think that the political agenda of the WCC and the NCC has hijacked ecumenism. Their political advocacy doesn't represent the people in the pews. I mean, I'm a supporter of the Christian Churches Together movement [CCT]. I've tirelessly worked within the National Association of Evangelicals to encourage those churches to get involved in the CCT.

ZH: The NCC supports and promotes Christian Churches Together. Have you publicly applauded them for that, or for any of the positive things that they're doing?

DK: I'd have to think about that, if I've done that recently. . .

ZH: What does it say about the IRD's credibility if all it ever says publicly about the NCC and the mainline churches is negative, judgmental and critical?

DK: [Long pause] Well, I think people will just have to judge that for themselves. I think that our criticisms have integrity. I think that the political agenda of, say, the NCC has just overwhelmed some of its other parts, such as the Faith and Order movement. I mean, I'm glad that the NCC supports the CCT. At the same time, I feel that if we're going to get the evangelical churches involved, the NCC's influence and control need to be minimized.

ZH: I read an interview that you did a year or so ago with the "Religion & Ethics" newsletter on the Christian/Muslim dialogue. I was impressed in that interview that you were promoting dialogue as a way to heal divisions. Yet, advocating dialogue doesn't seem to apply in the IRD's relationship with churches that it criticizes. Is there a different standard for dealing with other religions and with divisions within the Christian family?

DK: No, I think that dialogue rightly understood can be a helpful thing for bridging gaps. It can also be a manipulative tool.

ZH: How so? Give an example.

DK: Well, I think that's been the experience that many conservatives have had about dialogue over sexuality issues in the mainline churches. It's been a way to string people along, to make them feel like they are having a voice, but it doesn't really make any difference. It's just been a discouraging experience.

ZH: We're talking about lots of people's lives, though, when we're discussing sexuality. Isn't it worth investing time, even lots of time, if you're talking about people's relationship to the church, their vocations and their calling from God?

DK: Yes, and I've been involved in a sexuality dialogue in my diocese for seven years. I mean, we do certainly have lots of conversations with people. We interview people, we talk to people. I'm not opposed to the idea of dialogue.

ZH: In your interview with "Religion and Ethics" you state, "I'm sure that non-communication and mutual ignorance are not the way for peace in the world." That's a wonderful statement. Yet, the IRD is advocating division within The United Methodist Church, citing "irreconcilable differences" and inviting people to leave who don't agree with the church's positions on certain issues.

DK: Well, for one thing, we're talking about apples and oranges. We are concerned about dialogue with Muslims, but not so we can become part of one religious institution. In The United Methodist Church, we are not calling for the division of the church at all, but we are saying there are some individuals who for conscience's sake can no longer respect and abide by the doctrine and discipline of the UMC. We want to be generous with them. I mean, we can't force people out.

ZH: The IRD and those allied with it seem to be pursuing this agenda through what some would call legalism: Hold church trials and eliminate people with whom they disagree. Defrock an excellent lesbian pastor, for example, as the UMC recently did. What I'm wondering here is this: Are legalism, promoting division in the church and undermining the churches' leaders an expression of the Christian gospel in the IRD's view?

DK: I don't see that that's what we're doing at all. Look, if someone was guilty of sexual harassment in a business, and they were called to account for that because they violated the law, is that legalism?

ZH: You're talking about criminal behavior! Is that your comparison for somebody's sexual orientation and commitment to a loving relationship as a gay person?

DK: I would say that holding people accountable to the doctrine and discipline of the church is not legalism, it's integrity.

ZH: That's an interesting way to re-frame the issue, to call it "integrity" instead of legalism.

DK: You know, the New Testament is full of examples of Christians not living a life that is consistent with biblical standards and the teaching of the church, and the need for discipline. The overwhelming witness of the Christian church around the world and historically has been that God's intention is for human sexuality to be expressed in marriage between a man and a woman.

ZH: The overwhelming witness of the church through history has been patriarchal, too. It has reinforced, directly and indirectly, structures of male dominance. Does that make it right?

DK: You know, I believe that the Bible, biblical religion, Judaism and Christianity have done more to elevate the status of women than any other agency in human history. I'm not defending everything the church has done. Church councils can err. But I believe that, on the whole, the church has done more to elevate women.

ZH: I agree, which is another way of making the larger point: We don't have the same standard today on many issues-socially, culturally or even morally-that were held in biblical times.

DK: The existence of the evolution of doctrine or change does not justify every change. I mean, you wouldn't say, "OK, we've changed our position, and all of a sudden incest is O.K." I presume that you draw some lines.

ZH: Of course, including where exploitation is involved, which tends to be the case with incest.

DK: Not between an adult brother and sister.

ZH: In a male-dominant culture, incest tends to be a sin of exploitation, not a sin of sexual consent. Your comparison is revealing, though. The way the religious right frames the discussion regarding sex disturbs many of us because it says, in essence, there is nothing further to talk about when it comes to traditional views of sex, which means underlying issues such as exploitation and violence get ignored. So, the IRD's solution is that those who want to continue the dialogue should simply leave.

DK: Well, we cannot avoid the talk. The point about leaving is that if you cannot abide by the agreed doctrine and discipline of the church, we want to provide a generous way for people to exit and find a more congenial place.

ZH: Some might say that there's irony here, that the IRD advocates for freedom of religious expression outside the U.S.— in the Sudan for example—but that you balk at people wanting to practice their faith within their chosen denomination in the United States when they dissent with its teachings. Does that sound hypocritical to you?

DK: No, no, no, not at all. It's mixing of categories. Religious freedom is freedom from being coerced by the state. And we are absolutely for religious freedom for everyone. But religious freedom is not just the right of individuals. It is the right of religious institutions to maintain their own identity.

ZH: But, isn't there also the right of members to advocate for changing church policies? Why do mainline churches have regular general meetings to vote on such matters, for example, if there's not an understanding that these things can change?

DK: I think you have to pick and choose when things should change and when they shouldn't change. It seems to me that the doctrine of marriage and biblical teachings on human sexuality are very basic and, clearly, most United Methodists agree with that.

We're not forcing anyone out who disagrees. I mean, what about the one who was recently tried in Pennsylvania—Beth Stroud—I mean, she's still a United Methodist.

ZH: But Beth Stroud's vocation as one called by God to ordained service in the church has been taken away from her.

DK: Well, let's see. Your understanding and her understanding that she's called by God are clearly in question. I mean, perhaps she was called by God, but the advice of her bishop that she either lead a celibate lifestyle or pursue ordained ministry in another denomination—maybe that was God's word to her as well.

ZH: Apparently that advice wasn't included in the call as she heard it from God, though.

DK: You know, we can misunderstand God's call.

ZH: Have you ever considered that maybe the IRD has done just that?

DK: Oh, my goodness, yes. I am confident in what I believe, and I feel that I'm called to express these views and make these arguments publicly. Am I a sinner? Yes. Am I capable of misunderstanding God? Absolutely. I don't think we've ever tried to imply anything else.

ZH: How do you really feel in your heart of hearts about the defrocking of Beth Stroud?

DK: I feel that she was misled by people who were in spiritual authority over her about the teachings of The United Methodist Church and was encouraged in a direction she should not have gone.

ZH: Is the IRD going to try to hold those people accountable? Is the next move here to go after collaborators and people who support the Beth Strouds?

DK: Well, we don't have any plans right now. But, I do believe that bishops who don't uphold the teaching of the church are failing in their obligations. Now whether or not there's a mechanism for discipline of that sort in the UMC, I have no idea.

ZH: How about Beth herself?

DK: I can hope and pray that this will be an occasion and a means of grace for her, that she might find a way to re-embrace God's teaching on sexuality. Awful things can be a means of grace.

ZH: Have you ever once in public commended a liberal point of view?

DK: Well, most recently we did a press release regarding the UCC ad, suggesting that the media ought to be open to religious advertising and that, while clearly networks have the right to decide what they're going to advertise or not, we encouraged them to be open to religious advertising both liberal and conservative. We also encouraged the UCC to pull that particular ad because we thought that it was trying to boost their membership and view of inclusiveness at the expense of other churches.

ZH: So you would encourage the networks to run religious ads, but preferably only ones you approve?

DK: No, no. We encourage the networks to publish religious messages, knowing that we would approve or disapprove of them. We encouraged the UCC to withdraw this particular ad. Its message is that many churches are turning away people, but we, the UCC, welcome people. Well, give me a break! Churches don't have bouncers like the ad showed. You know, the UCC doesn't get this award for being the most welcoming denomination. That's what we were objecting to. We thought it was an un-ecumenical ad, trying to boost their numbers by stereotyping other churches.

ZH: Has the IRD ever opposed any U.S. military action?

DK: [long pause] Not that I can recall, nor have we endorsed it. In fact, I was invited by Richard Land [of the Southern Baptist Ethics and Religious Liberty Commission] to endorse the war in Iraq, and I declined to do that.

ZH: That's rather disingenuous, though, when you consider that all of the IRD's statements regarding the Iraq war have been critical of those churches, and those in the church, who have opposed the war.

DK: You know, we did a pretty sophisticated and careful argument for why we felt that church leaders were wrong in...Let me just back up, because a lot of people misunderstand this. People assume that when we criticize the church for doing something, that means we want the church to do the opposite. A lot of times we just believe that church leaders should be a little more modest and careful and a little less inclined to speak on every political issue that comes down the road.

ZH: But don't you see that, when the whole weight of your public statements goes in just one direction, it doesn't take a real bright mind to figure out what you actually support?

DK: But, you know, again, we do not want...we are not about trying to replace the left-leaning social-political witness of the mainline churches with a right-leaning or Republican witness. We believe that the churches, on many issues, should be more modest and should respect differences of opinion within the church on those issues. You know, for example on the issue of war, we do support "just war." We're not a pacifist organization. We believe it is up to church leaders to teach "just war" theory. It's up to people in government to apply "just war" teaching.

ZH: I recall numerous objections to the Iraq war based precisely on "just war" theory, some appearing in this magazine, including how the war failed the test of "last resort." I don't recall seeing a single affirmation of any of those efforts from the IRD.

DK: I would need to know specifically what you're talking about.

ZH: But did you affirm any of them?

DK: No.

ZH: Much of the emphasis of the IRD is on the importance of doctrine in the church and the adherence to doctrine. Do you really believe that doctrine is the make-or-break issue for a Christian, that we're saved by our belief in doctrine?

DK: No, we're saved by the gracious mercy of Jesus Christ and His sacrificial death for us. Right doctrine is, however, very important. I would say it's essential for preserving the faith. It is the duty of the church and church leaders to preserve right doctrine because it's our understanding of who God is and how God relates to us.

ZH: For Christians in the Wesleyan tradition, the matter is viewed as a bit more complex than that, I think. Hence, the tests of Scripture, tradition, reason and experience as applied to our "understanding of God." Why must we define only one set of teachings as being "right" when the test of experience, for example, might lead one to another conclusion?

DK: Well, for one thing, my understanding is that when Wesley was talking about experience it wasn't just general life experience. It was experience with the Holy Spirit. And I think that the Holy Spirit does not lead us in ways that contradict Scripture. Now, Wesley talked about the Wesleyan Quadrilateral, and that's important. But he also had the Articles of Religion. Wesley had fundamental doctrines. I can't imagine that Wesley would have remotely suggested that, for example, the ancient creeds of the church would be up for grabs and re-writing.

ZH: Yet Wesley apparently had a spiritual experience that revealed the wrongness of slavery, which flew in the face of the church's tradition and its reading of the scripture during his time. You say the Holy Spirit is never in contradiction with scripture, but clearly it sometimes is.

DK: I don't believe it is. I think that there have been times when the church misunderstood Scripture. If I feel that the Spirit is telling me something, well, how do you test the Spirit? You test the Spirit by going to Scripture. You also test the Spirit by going to the witness of the whole church.

ZH: What motivates you? Where does your passion come from?

DK: Well, I desperately want to see strong, healthy, orthodox, growing churches in our society. I went to Asbury College and I'm really grateful for my experience there in the Wesleyan holiness movement, because I could have gone in another direction. Also, my father was in the military when I was growing up, and I lived abroad. That international experiences shaped me and made me very interested in foreign policy and politics.

ZH: On an even more personal note, you have publicly shared information about your illness. What can you tell us about that now? How are you?

DK: Well, I'm in chemotherapy right now, and I don't know what the future is. I first was diagnosed with cancer on my 31st wedding anniversary. My advice is, don't go get the colonoscopy on your anniversary…but do get the colonoscopy! I've always been remarkably healthy, so the first thing you think is, "You know, this isn't me. This couldn't be me." But my husband and I from the very beginning prayed that God would be glorified. I don't know what the outcome will be. I could be healed. I could continue in therapy. I could die in the next few years. But I also believe that God works through all things for good for those who love him. I'm not sure I would trade all the spiritual lessons I've learned. In some respects, it has been humbling because you need other people. You need their help. There are things you can't do. I've realized that, because I've been so healthy that probably I haven't been as sympathetic to people who suffer illness. And I've vowed to do better. And I'm just amazed by the medical profession, too. I've seen a side of our culture that I've not seen before.

ZH: We'll keep you in our prayers.
DK: Thank you.

———————

EDITOR'S NOTE

Diane Knippers died while this volume was being prepared for publication. Although we were aware of her illness, as our final exchange indicated, her death nevertheless came as a shock to those of us who were her professional colleagues and, not infrequently, her adversaries during the past 25 years. Despite our many differences and conflicting interpretations of the Christian faith, Diane was unfailingly gracious and respectful whenever circumstances brought us together.

As we began the above interview, I prefaced it by telling Diane that my intent, among other things, was to be "aggressive but not hostile" in asking questions on behalf of our publication's readers. She readily agreed to those terms and conducted herself with composure and sturdy conviction. After what indeed proved to be a strenuous engagement of our differing viewpoints, she thanked me for the experience and wondered aloud why we didn't do "this sort of thing more often." I was impressed!

As I've thought about her final musing that day, it is clear to me that, indeed, we *should* do "this sort of thing more often." It saddens me that she and I will not have the opportunity to do so again on this side of eternity. But in some respects this volume, with its "give and take" interplay among Christians deeply divided over matters of faith, is a fitting follow-up to her sentiment.

Stealthy Zinger

STEPHEN SWECKER

I n the whole history of the American church, there's perhaps
never been anything quite like the Institute on Religion and
Democracy. That's stated with a certain grudging respect. I
don't like what the IRD stands for or does, but its impact on
mainline Protestant churches—primarily Episcopalian,
Presbyterian and United Methodist—is undeniable. Against all
likelihood, it has become a significant player at the intersection of
politics and religion. With the 2004 election of the neoconserva-
tive-backed George W. Bush, the IRD's influence perhaps has
never been greater since its inception 23 years ago.

The fact that a typical member of a mainline church could not
tell you much, if anything, about the IRD, including what its ini-
tials stand for, is paradoxical evidence of its success. For the
most part, it has been a stealth operator, working to discredit
church leaders, roil congregations and provoke conflict without
drawing other than glancing attention to itself. What's more,
being independent of church structures, it is impervious to criti-

cism from those whom it critiques, including bishops and church executives.

For this reason, the IRD often succeeds at what it aims to do, namely, stir suspicion among church folk that something's rotten in the ecclesiastical ranks. Using a variety of tactics, it's conceivable that the IRD has done more in this regard to poison the well of Christian community in the U.S. than any other organization, past or present.

That's why it distresses me when otherwise responsible publications give the IRD unmerited credibility—unmerited because the nine-member IRD staff speaks solely for itself and reports only to its own self-appointed, right-leaning 19-member board of directors. It never answers to the court of public opinion for the quality of its work, its unbalanced reporting or its often sophomoric analyses of complex topics.

For example, when New York Times religion editor Peter Steinfels recently turned to the IRD for a comment on the United Church of Christ/TV ad controversy, he got exactly what he had to know he would: criticism of the UCC. Shocking! But that's the IRD's stock-in-trade: provide a predictable source of sound-bite criticism of mainline Christians. It's one-stop shopping for mainline zingers. It's also lazy journalism. (Sorry, Peter.)

So, what exactly is the IRD? Its effects are easy enough to describe, but where does it fit in the bigger context of forces at work in our society? In broad strokes, this much seems evident:

The IRD is an amateurish political expression of a 20th-century movement known as "deconstructionism." Simplified, deconstructionists seek to expose the shadow side of structures—literary, social, artistic—anything whose "construction" can be broken down into component parts and its hidden dimensions revealed. Employed responsibly, deconstructionists in many fields have clarified aspects of experience, often creatively, that are obscured by conventional ways of seeing and thinking.

Turned upon the church, for example, deconstruction helps to expose its sad history of racial injustice and abuse of male power. Used solely in this manner, however, to show only the underside, deconstruction no doubt could draw a portrait of Christianity—or any religion or institution, for that matter—as a hideous distortion of the human spirit.

In the IRD's hands, this is precisely the effect. It seeks to deconstruct the church's leadership, particularly the latter's social witness against injustice and its advocacy for the power-less. Framing its concerns as "integrity" and "accountability," the IRD relentlessly attacks (their word is "monitor") bishops, pas-tors, church executives and denominational programs in what has been described as an endless game of "gotcha."

Its ostensible goal is the restoration and enforcement of a 5th-century form of church doctrine, which it calls Orthodoxy. This extends to insisting on adherence to specific ancient creeds and teachings lest one be cast into the darkness (or simply asked to leave, today's genteel version of excommunication). Taking a chapter from church espionage of a darker era, the IRD actually sends staff to worship services and meetings of suspect groups to record (and afterwards denounce) deviations from its Orthodox agenda.

Unsurprisingly, the IRD does not bother to deconstruct its brand of Orthodoxy and its wealthy backers. Were it to do so, it would have to reveal its Constantinian character, reminiscent of the church's unholy alliance with the Roman state shaped by the 4th-century convert, Emperor Constantine. At the very least, this would clarify the IRD's uncritical relationship with the powers that be, political and corporate. Not only has the IRD influenced voters that put them in power, but it gets lots of its money from the same coffers. In return, for starters, it never criticizes the U.S. military or corporate America.

The individuals who work for the IRD appear to me to be authentic. That is, they truly believe in what they do and, in per-sonal interactions, are civil, even gracious. Their efforts to pro-mote the IRD's religious liberty program, although a relatively small part of their work, appear well-intended.

103

History, however, will repudiate the IRD and its spiritual kin. As their tactics and goals become exposed, they will be seen for what they are: reactionary instruments of a broader effort to turn back the clock on inexorable advances by church and society in the pursuit of truth, freedom and justice. In the end, the IRD is not a program grounded in faith but, rather, in fear–both fear of change in general and fear of loss by those who benefit most from the *status quo*, i.e., the wealthy and the powerful.

If a gain can be claimed by mainline Christians in response to the challenge posed by the IRD, it will be to construct and practice a mature political spirituality grounded in love of God and neighbor. Such a spirituality will be equipped to discern how the likes of the IRD fall short of a Gospel vision for life together on Earth. It also will help heal the corrosive impact they have had on the mainline community of faith, an impact whose depths we are just beginning to comprehend. Finally, a mature political spirituality will strengthen our evolving witness as Jesus' followers called to be light for the world and agents of an authentic, life-giving interplay between religion and democracy.

CONTRIBUTORS

Scott Campbell is Senior Minister of Harvard-Epworth United Methodist Church in Cambridge, Massachusetts and a regular columnist for Zion's Herald.

John B. Cobb, Jr., Ph.D., is Professor of Theology Emeritus at the Claremont School of Theology, Claremont, California.

Thom White Wolf Fassett is a former General Secretary of the General Board of Church and Society of The United Methodist Church and a District Superintendent in upstate New York.

Fred W. Kandeler, M.Div., D.D., is a retired United Methodist pastor affiliated with Travis Park UMC, San Antonio, Texas.

Diane Knippers is the former President of the Institute on Religion and Democracy. Ms. Knippers died during the preparation of this volume, on April 18, 2005.

Linda S. Rhodes is Editor of The Reporter of the Northern Illinois Conference of The United Methodist Church.

Nicole Seibert, B. A., is a United Methodist layperson and an instructor of sociology at Alfred State College in upstate New York.

Stephen Swecker is Editor of Zion's Herald and Editor-in-Chief of BW Press.

Mark Tooley is director of the IRD's UM Action Committee.

Andrew J. Weaver, M.Th., Ph.D., is a United Methodist pastor, research psychologist and Associate Publisher of Zion's Herald.

J. Philip Wogaman, Ph. D., is Interim President of Iliff Theological Seminary and President of the American Theological Society.

How To Order More Copies
Of *HARD BALL ON HOLY GROUND*

ONLINE
www.amazon.com

or

www.booksurge.com

TELEPHONE
Toll Free: 1-866-308-6235

Hard Ball on Holy Ground

983421